A
BRIEF
INTRODUCTION TO
SPEECH

SECOND EDITION

A
BRIEF
INTRODUCTION TO
SPEECH

SECOND EDITION

Donovan J. Ochs

The University of Iowa

Anthony C. Winkler

Harcourt Brace Jovanovich, Inc.

New York • San Diego • Chicago • San Francisco • Atlanta

London • Sydney • Toronto

Requests for permission to make copies of any part of the work should
be mailed to: Permissions, Harcourt Brace Jovanovich, Publishers, 757
Third Avenue, New York, NY 10017.

ISBN: 0-15-505585-2
Library of Congress Catalog Card Number: 82-083814
Printed in the United States of America

COPYRIGHTS AND ACKNOWLEDGMENTS

For permission to use the selections reprinted in this book, the authors are grateful to the following
publishers and copyright holders:

CITY NEWS PUBLISHING CO.   For excerpt from "Who Is Tampering with the Soul of
America?" by Jenkins Lloyd Jones. Reprinted in *Vital Speeches of the Day*, January 1, 1962.
Used with permission of City News Publishing Co.

EDUCATIONAL FOUNDATION FOR NUCLEAR SCIENCE   For "Preventing Nuclear War" by
Roger Fisher. Reprinted by permission of *The Bulletin of the Atomic Scientists*, a magazine of
science and public affairs. Copyright © 1981 by the Educational Foundation for Nuclear
Science, Chicago, Ill., 60637.

HOUGHTON MIFFLIN COMPANY   For excerpt from *On Becoming a Person* by Carl R.
Rogers. Copyright © 1961 by Carl R. Rogers. Reprinted by permission of Houghton Mifflin
Company.

INTERSTATE ORATORICAL ASSOCIATION   For excerpts from "Madame Butterfly and the
Collegian," 1967, by Patricia Ann Hayes; "Bring Forth the Children," 1971, by Patricia Warren;
"Mingled Blood," 1956, by Ralph Zimmerman. All reprinted by permission of the Interstate
Oratorical Association.

ALFRED A. KNOPF, INC.   For excerpt from *Resistance, Rebellion, and Death* by Albert Camus,
translated by Justin O'Brien. Copyright © 1960 by Alfred A. Knopf, Inc. Reprinted by
permission of the publisher.

WIL A. LINKUGEL   For excerpts from "The Unmentionable Disease" by Mary K. Wayman in
Contemporary American Speeches, Second Edition. Copyright © 1969 by Wadsworth Publishing Company, Inc. Reprinted by permission of the authors, Linkugel, Allen, and Johannesen.

PREFACE

The second edition of *A Brief Introduction to Speech*, like the first, is written for the beginning student of public speaking. The emphasis in this edition, as in the previous one, is on the similarities and differences between talking and *presenting a speech*, between writing and *speaking*, and between reading and *doing research for a speech*.

However, the second edition of *A Brief Introduction to Speech* has been completely restructured. Each chapter is now divided into three sections: "*Principles*," "*Applications*," and "*Cautions*." Under "*Principles*," we cover the basic theories and ideas of a topic; under "*Applications*," we show students how to apply these ideas to their own speechmaking; under "*Cautions*," we warn against common errors. Each section ends with a capsule review of the material covered in it.

This systematic treatment of principles, applications, and cautions permits us to isolate and identify those theories, practices, and caveats that are important for students to understand if they are to become better public speakers. Pedagogically, the arrangement allows students to turn directly to the parts of a topic that they are weakest in, while the text as a whole demonstrates the important and realistic relationship between the theory and practice of public speaking.

We have also made other changes in this edition. Chapter 4, "Adapting to an Audience," is entirely new. Chapter 6, "Gathering Materials," has been completely rewritten to cover more than library sources. To Chapter 13, "The Speech to Inform," we have added a section on narrative speaking, and to Chapter 14, "The Speech to Persuade," we have added a section defining what is an arguable issue. All other chapters have been updated, and most chapters now end with a brief list of works for further reading.

Though it contains more material, *A Brief Introduction to Speech,* Second Edition, continues to be compact and readable. Now it is also arranged to fit the circumstances of the classroom and the demands for pragmatic, to-the-point coverage of the essentials of public speaking.

CONTENTS

3 Coping with speechfright

27

4 Adapting to an audience

39

PART 2 SPEECH PREPARATION AND DELIVERY

49

5 The topic and the central idea

 51

6 Gathering materials   65

7 How to use supporting details   79

PART 3 GENERAL TYPES OF SPEECHES

13 The speech to inform

14 The speech to persuade

Index   233

SPEAKERS
AND
LISTENERS

1

Contexts and norms of public speaking

I. PRINCIPLES

Human beings are not the only animals to use sounds in their daily lives. But humans seem to be the only ones who use sounds to communicate *symbolically*—that is, to stand for ideas, intentions, feelings, and things. How they do this is better known than why.

What is known, however, is that for a person to utter even a simple greeting like "How are you today?" requires the complex interplay of four physical structures: lungs that act as a bellows; a sound generator in the larynx (the so-called vocal cords); a sound resonator in the pharynx (a cone-shaped tube about 4½ inches long that runs through the mouth and nasal passages); and the oral cavity, or mouth, in which the sounds are finally shaped and formed. The speaker expands the thoracic cavity through the use of either the diaphragm or the chest muscles, increasing the volume of the lungs. Air flows into the lungs in response to greater air pressure as the person inhales.

A person who means merely to take a breath and not to talk would typically breathe at the rate of eighteen to twenty times a minute, absorbing and giving off approximately one pint of air. But inhalation is greater during speech—involving one to two quarts of air—and breath is expelled at a force nearly one hundred times stronger. Air rushes out of the lungs, causing the membranes in the larynx to vibrate and pulse out sound waves at nearly 1200 feet per second. The waves resonate against the hard structures of the teeth, the palate, and the bone of the nose, giving a distinctive color to the sound which is then articulated by the movement of the mouth.

On the receiving end of these sound waves is the ear, an organ whose mechanism is not completely understood. Sound waves enter the auditory canal and strike the eardrum, setting up vibrations which travel along the auditory nerve as signals to the brain. How the brain translates these signals into the greeting "How are you today?" remains a mystery. We also don't know how the brain distinguishes low-pitched sounds from high-pitched sounds or how it differentiates between loud sounds and soft sounds. In any case, this simple greeting delivered by, say, one commuter to another at a bus stop has involved a physiological sequence of staggering complexity that we take quite for granted.

But even the simplest oral communication between humans entails more than merely a larynx talking to an eardrum. It involves a speaker and a listener, both of whom are individual personalities; each has a cultural background, unique experiences, and a particular way of looking at the world. The variables involved between speaker and listener may be diagramatically represented as follows:

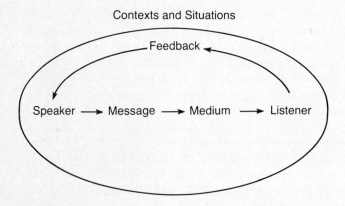

There is a speaker, who *encodes* (delivers) the message; a listener, who *decodes* (hears and interprets) it; a *medium* through which the message is transmitted; and the various contexts in which the message exists, is delivered, and is interpreted. In the case of the two commuters exchanging a greeting at a bus stop, the speaker is one commuter; the listener is another; and the transmitting medium is the air.

The diagram shows, too, that the message of any communication is also affected by *contexts* of time, place, and personalities.

All oral messages exist in time—in a unique historical moment that affects the interpretation of symbols. In 1975, if you had tried to express your passionately held views on the neutron bomb you would have had a difficult time making yourself understood because the existence of the bomb was not then part of the public consciousness. *Vietnam* is a word that can be uttered today without the same feverish meaning that it had during the height of the war. *Inflation* meant one thing to people in the 1950s, when the cost-of-living index was an anemic 3 percent; it means quite another to people in the 1980s, when it rages at about 17 percent. The meanings and connotations that words have are mutually agreed upon from one era to another, are subject to shifts in values, and are constantly undergoing subtle changes in response to changes in the human condition.

Oral messages are also subject to the vagaries of the physical place in which the communication is attempted. When our two commuters met at the bus stop, presumably they shared a quiet moment in which a greeting could be exchanged. However, if a jackhammer had been operating ten feet away from them, the greeting would perhaps have consisted merely of eye contact and a nod. If a blizzard were raging all around them, "How are you today?" might seem sarcastic or frivolous rather than friendly. It is a trite but true observation that the physical setting in which an oral message was delivered can also affect its meaning.

Communication is further complicated by the unique context of every human life. We are all conditioned by a particular set of experiences that have shaped our views of the world and affect the personal meanings we attach to words. Clyde Kluckhohn, late Harvard professor of anthropology, used to tell the story of a teacher who complained that her Navajo students were socially backward and cited as an example her inability to get them even to dance at a high school prom. It turned out that she was urging members of the same clan to dance with each other—which, in the Navajo culture, amounted to incest. The harmless greeting "How are you today?" cannot have the same meaning for the person secretly stricken with terminal cancer as for the healthy person. This is an extreme example, but it illustrates an important principle: because no two people are exactly alike, we do not respond in exactly the same way to the same words.

Review of principles

To review the principles covered in this chapter: human beings seem to be the only animals to use speech symbolically. Speaking is a complicated physiological act that makes use of four organs: the lungs, the larynx, the pharynx, and the mouth. Communication involves a speaker, who encodes (delivers) a message; a transmitting medium; and a decoding listener, who interprets the message. In any communication there is a context of time and place that is shared by the speaker and the listener. Yet both speaker and listener bring to the act of communication their unique experiences that influence their individual interpretation of words. Sensitive communicators take into account the attitudes and experiences of their listeners.

II. APPLICATIONS

Speaking and talking

Public speaking is a special kind of communication involving one person talking to many. And it is the kind of communication with which students usually have had no practice. Yet by the time you are old enough to read this book, you will have already logged thousands of hours of personal conversation but perhaps only a few minutes of public speaking. So a useful place to begin the study of public speaking is to contrast it with the oral communication you're already familiar with: namely, conversation.

To start with, many of the skills you use in private conversation are the same as those you would use in a speech. Consider, for instance, a simple conversation with a friend. You say something; the friend responds; you evaluate the response and make a reply. Moreover, during the course of your talk, you probably automatically adapt your vocabulary and syntax to match the level of the person you're talking to.

If you were giving a speech before an audience, you would make similar adaptations, but with some premeditation. You would take into account the audience you intend to address, selecting a subject you think would appeal to them and expressing it in language you think they would understand. If the audience started yawning during your speech, you would realize that you were boring them and adjust your presentation to make it more interesting.

So far the two kinds of communication—the conversation and

the public speech—do not seem especially different. Yet there are significant differences between them.

First, a public speaker cannot address an audience in the same soft tone of voice that could be used in conversation. The speaker must use helpful gestures, talk in a strong and clear voice, and generally employ an emphatic and heightened delivery in order to be seen, heard, and understood. This may be why public speakers are sometimes regarded as "stagy." Good public speakers, however, are never "hams." They know how to intensify their voice and presence before an audience while preserving their dignity and their sense of self.

Second, complex ideas are more readily explained and more easily understood in a one-to-one talk than in a formal public speech. There are exceptions, but public speakers generally do not try to explain abstract or complex notions. Subtleties, faint shades of meaning and ambiguities do not generally fare well in speeches. Instead, speeches are usually structured and developed around one or two primary ideas that are carefully stated, restated, and amplified.

In a way, formal speechmaking is to personal conversation what the breaststroke is to the backstroke. Both strokes are used in swimming; both speechmaking and casual talking are forms of communication. The swimmer who knows how to swim one stroke can readily learn the other. Likewise, the student who has spent two or three decades talking can learn to give formal speeches, and give them well.

Norms of speaking

Human behavior is governed by norms—standards of acceptability which most people obey in various degrees. Whether we eat with a fork or use our fingers is determined by the norm we have been taught to observe. Norms certainly govern our use of language. Football players during a game do not use the same type of language as townspeople at a civic meeting. In some circles it is the norm to say *ain't;* in others, *ain't* is regarded with horror.

Public speaking too has its accepted standards. Among them are the following:

1. A speaker must adapt the subject matter to the audience

Audiences, like people in general, vary. Some have long attention spans, some have short attention spans; some are highly educated, some are poorly educated; some are interested in birdwatching, some in bird-shooting. The same speech is not likely to appeal to all. Good speakers therefore adapt the subject matter of their speeches to suit their audiences. This adaptation may affect the speaker's diction, choice of supporting material, and length of sentences. The aim is not to pander to an audience but to make one's ideas understood.

2. A speaker must anticipate an audience's questions

In a personal conversation, the speakers can easily interrupt one another to ask a question; members of an audience seldom have a similar opportunity with a speaker. A speaker must therefore anticipate the questions an audience might ask and attempt to answer them in the speech. For example, if you were giving a speech about the causes of air pollution, you might anticipate your audience's questions about what could be done to combat pollution and include some answers in the text of the speech. The questions that might occur to an audience will depend, of course, on the subject matter of the speech and on the nature of the audience. That is why it is important for a speaker to be as familiar with the audience as with the topic.

3. The speaker must address an audience's needs, not its wants

An audience of homeowners gathered together to oppose a property-tax increase may *need* to be told why their taxes must either go up or their community services go down. What the same audience will no doubt *want* to hear is a denunciation of all tax increases. However, an ethical speaker with a different point of view will not simply cave in to the audience's desires. Instead, ethical speakers try to educate an audience by giving them information they *need* rather than merely telling them what they *want* to hear.

4. The speaker must support claims made in the speech

Support refers to the information and evidence that back up a speaker's assertions. Some speeches make no claims and therefore need no support. But other speeches make assertions—for example, that the property tax must be raised. When the assertion is in dispute, the speaker must include figures, facts, testimonials, and reasons to show that the claims made are believable and justified. (For more on this topic, see Chapters 2 and 7.)

5. The speaker must establish trustworthiness with the audience

What makes one speaker believable and another not is an age-old question. Aristotle (384–322 B.C.) attempted to answer it with his explanation of *ethos*—the Greek word for character. Basically, Aristotle theorized that whether an audience trusted a speaker depended on their perception of the speaker's character. Subsequent research has more or less confirmed Aristotle's theory (see Chapter 14). It boils down to this: speakers who wish to be believed have to establish themselves as trustworthy in the eyes of the audience. How this is done is a matter of some debate which we will look at in greater detail in Chapter 14. For the time being, we can say that if you gave a speech in which you observed all the norms mentioned here but this one, you probably still wouldn't be believed if the audience perceived you as untrustworthy.

Review of applications

Your ability to carry on personal conversations can stand you in good stead in public speaking. But as a public speaker you also need to intensify your manner so that your message will carry and be understandable to your audience. Complex and technical ideas generally do not fare well in a public speech; instead, you must structure your speech around one or two main ideas that are stated, restated, and amplified.

Just as there are norms of grammar that apply to writing, there are also norms that apply to speechmaking. These norms include the requirement that a speaker adapt the subject matter to the level of the audience; anticipate an audience's questions; address an audience's needs rather than their wants; include support for any disputed assertions; and establish trust in the minds of the audience.

III. CAUTIONS

Many similarities exist between conversation and public speaking, but so do a number of significant differences. Only on the rarest occasions do we *prepare* for private conversation. Public speaking, on the other hand, is usually a premeditated business. When we sit down to exchange our views of the world with a friend, we don't plan what we're going to say. But if we intend to present information sensibly to an audience in a speech, we have to structure the facts and ideas we'll be using. We may be as homespun or as idiomatic as we please in a personal conversation and use any number of private references so long as they are shared by our listener. In a public speech, though, we must use only words, terms, and references that will be readily understandable to strangers.

The most elementary caution, then, for the beginning speaker is summed up in the Boy Scout motto: "Be prepared." Find out what you can about your audience and incorporate this information in the preparation of your speech. Do not simply assume that because you think of yourself as basically a decent sort you can stand up at a podium and everyone will see your sterling qualities. Know your audience; know your subject; plan your speech so that it appeals to the needs of your audience.

A second caution is to build redundancy and repetition into the major points of your speech. Beginning speakers tend to forget that the eye is not only quicker than the ear, but it also has the advantage of pause and playback. If you didn't understand this last sentence, for example, you can simply reread it. Listeners can't do that. The good speaker will therefore usually amplify all the major points so as to give listeners a second or even a third chance to understand them. Sometimes repetition is used for emphasis or persuasive appeal. But often it simply helps listeners follow the major points of the speech.

A third caution is to be sensitive to *feedback* from the audience. Feedback refers to verbal and nonverbal cues that tell you how the audience is responding to your speech. A sea of eyes glued with rapture to your face may indicate that your speech is a hit. An epidemic of shuffling, coughing, and yawning, should tell you something else. The alert speaker is always ready to change a presentation if it is obvious that the speech isn't getting through to the audience.

Finally, you should speak in an audible voice and refrain from using any mannerisms that are likely to distract from your words. It is difficult for any audience to concentrate on a speech when the speaker has an annoying delivery habit that draws attention to itself. Ideally your delivery should allow the audience to focus on your ideas rather than on your speaking mechanics.

Review of cautions

Our first caution for the beginning speaker is: "Be prepared." Know your subject matter; know your audience; adapt your speech to appeal to their needs. You are also cautioned to build redundancy and repetition into your speech, to be sensitive to audience feedback during the speech, and to deliver the speech in an audible voice free of any irritating delivery mannerisms.

FOR FURTHER READING

Aristotle. *The "Art" of Rhetoric.* Trans. John Henry Freese. Cambridge: Harvard University Press, 1975.

Becker, Samuel, and Ekdom, Leah. "The Forgotten Basic Skill: Oral Communication." *Iowa Journal of Speech Communication,* 12 (1980):1–8.

Cronkhite, Gary. *Communication and Awareness.* Menlo Park, Calif.: Cummings, 1976.

Dance, Frank E. X., and Larson, Carl E. *The Functions of Human Communication: A Theoretical Approach.* New York: Holt, Rinehart & Winston, 1976.

Gibson, James W., and Cornwell, Clifton. *Creative Speech Communication.* New York: Macmillan, 1979.

Harper, Nancy. *Human Communication Theory: The History of a Paradigm.* Rochelle Park, N.J.: Hayden, 1979.

McCroskey, James C., and Wheeless, Lawrence R. *Introduction to Human Communication.* Boston: Allyn & Bacon, 1976.

Searle, John R. *Speech Acts: An Essay in the Philosophy of Language.* New York: Cambridge University Press, 1969.

Wilson, John Rowan. *The Mind.* New York: Time-Life Books, 1964.

Listening

I. PRINCIPLES

Most of us think of listening as a simple process that comes naturally to everyone. However, research has shown that the act of listening is not as simple as we may think. It is divisible into at least four separate components: receiving, attending, assigning meaning, and remembering.[1] *Receiving* refers to the actual physiological process of listening; *attending,* to the listener's focus on a specific sound; *assigning meaning,* to the process by which our brains interpret the message; and *remembering,* to the storing of a message for later recall.[2] Listening is further classified by researchers into its different purposes: appreciative, discriminative, comprehensive, therapeutic, and critical. *Appreciative listening* is listening for enjoyment, as when we listen to music. *Discriminative listening* occurs when we try to distinguish between two very similar sounds—such as a parent listening to differentiate between the fussy and the hungry cries of an infant. *Comprehensive listening* is listening primarily for the purpose of understanding—like listening to a lecture. *Therapeutic listening* occurs when we listen sympathetically to a friend who wants to blow off steam. Finally, *critical listening* enables us to evaluate and judge a message.[3] All of us, at one time or another during the course of the day, will probably engage in all these different kinds of listening. And, for the most part, we do so ineffectively.

Indeed, according to the best available research, most of us are bad listeners. Typically we understand only one-half of what we listen to; after two months, we can recall only one-quarter of it. Yet it has been estimated that we spend 70 percent of every day in verbal communication. Of this, 9 percent is spent in writing, 16 percent in reading, 30 percent in talking, and 45 percent in listening.[4] It is also estimated that we draw 60 percent of our ideas from radio and television—media that rely heavily on listening.[5] One survey, conducted during a national election, revealed that the electorate had received only 27 percent of their information on the candidates and the issues from newspapers and magazines, and 58 percent from radio and television.[6] Listening not only bears the brunt of our day-to-day communication; it is also the primary skill we use in forming our political and general opinions.

Why are most of us such ineffective listeners? Many explanations have been offered, but the one that seems to have the most validity points to the considerable lag between the rate at which we speak and the rate at which we listen. Most people speak at a rate between 120 and 180 words per minute; the mind, however, can comprehend at a substantially faster rate—up to 600 words per minute or more. The theory is that the typical listener becomes bored and starts daydreaming while waiting for the speaker to catch up.

Another explanation contends that most of us are victims of bad listening habits acquired in our day-to-day contacts. The vast majority of us spend more time listening to personal conversations than to formal lectures and, aside from those rare moments of crisis, personal conversation does not promote attentive listening. Indeed, the very casualness of a friendly conversation may not only encourage but demand an easygoing approach to listening that can reinforce bad listening habits.

Some other observations can be made about listening. The first is that listening is an acquired, not an inherited, skill and does not correlate significantly with intelligence. The second observation is that listening behavior is affected by a variety of irrelevant stimuli. For example, listeners often dismiss the message of a speaker out-of-hand simply because they do not like the speaker's looks. The impulse to evaluate a message according to whether or not we like the speaker's looks has ancient origins. The Greek philosopher Diogenes (c. 412–323 B.C.) was ridiculed because he went about dressed in rags. And innumerable prophets were regarded as eccentric because they dressed differently from the people around them.

The third observation is that listening is often affected by the physical environment in which it takes place. Crammed into a crowded church pew in 100-degree weather, even a saint would have trouble paying attention to the minister. If intelligent listening is to take place, listeners must be comfortable. If they aren't, they will squirm, fidget, and daydream rather than listen.

However, no matter what explanations are given for poor listening, it is obvious that widespread reliance on a skill so ineffectively practiced must inevitably cause misunderstanding, confusion, and even disaster. The worst aircraft accident in history, a collision between two jumbo jets in the Canary Islands that took the lives of 582 people, has been blamed on faulty pilot listening. One of the worst peacetime disasters at sea was the sinking of the *Titanic* in 1912 after she failed to heed radio warnings of icebergs in her path.

There can also be grave consequences for any democracy whose citizens don't listen carefully. Bertrand Russell describes how Sidney Webb, a British socialist and prime mover in the early years of the British Labor Party, used to get his way in committees:

> . . . when he wished to carry some point through a committee where the majority thought otherwise, he would draw up a resolution in which the contentious point occurred twice. He would have a long debate about its first occurrence and at last give way graciously. Nine times out of ten, so he concluded, no one would notice that the same point occurred later in the same resolution.[7]

Ineffective listening by the electorate can even subject a nation to political catastrophe. An eyewitness to several of Hitler's speeches wrote that when Hitler was finished speaking "even the most level-headed listeners declared that, though they were still against the speaker and his party, Hitler himself was obviously much more reasonable than they had imagined."[8]

What constitutes effective listening? First, effective listening is active, not passive. The effective listener uses the lag in the rate between speaking and listening to paraphrase and evaluate what the speaker is saying. Second, effective listening requires a suspension of disbelief in the listener. "Suspension of disbelief" is most commonly used to describe the attitude a theatrical audience must consciously adopt during the performance of a play, but the phrase can apply as well to any listener. We are likely to miss a good deal of what speakers are saying if we mentally argue with them during the course of a speech. Finally, to listen effectively we must evaluate not only the speaker's words but also the appeals implicit in the speech (see Chapter 14). Listeners who consciously observe these three guidelines will inevitably hear and understand more than those who do not.

Review of principles

Most of us are unskilled listeners. We understand only about one-half of what we listen to, and after two months can usually recall only one-quarter of it. Yet we derive the greater part of our opinions from the "listening" media—radio and television. Several explanations for ineffective listening have been given; the most apparently valid one points to the lag between the rates of speaking and comprehension. Another explanation is that we pick up bad listening habits in casual conversations. Listening is affected by the physical environment in which it takes place and by the listener's judgment of the speaker's appearance. Efficient listening is an acquired skill that does not correlate significantly with intelligence. Efficient listening is active, involves a conscious suspension of disbelief, and requires the evaluation not only of a speaker's words but also of the appeals implicit in the speech.

II. APPLICATIONS

Your listening effectiveness can be markedly improved if you are willing to work at listening. But improvement will not come easily. You should get into the habit of consciously and actively listening rather than simply lapsing into the relaxed state of the casual listener. Our suggestions on how you can improve your listening fall into two categories: how to listen, and what to listen for.

How to listen

1. Prepare yourself to listen

Concentrate on the process of listening. Mentally blot out any noise, movement, or other distraction that may interfere with your listening. Try to find a seat or location that suits you. Make whatever comfort adjustments you have to before the speech begins. Listen to the introduction to the speaker. Analyze the speaker's credentials. Ask yourself whether you have any strong opinions on the speaker's topic and be prepared to suspend these temporarily during the course of the speech.

2. Take advantage of the lag between the rate of listening and speaking

Use the difference in the two rates to mentally paraphrase and evaluate the speaker's message. Pay attention to what the speaker is assuming, stressing, and omitting. Check the speaker's assertions against you own experiences. Examine the evidence the speaker uses. In short, be active and alert during the lag between the rates of speaking and listening.

3. Take notes

Note-taking is one way to occupy a mind that is threatening to outrace a speaker. In addition, it leaves you with a record that you can critically review after the speech is over. There are numerous forms of note-taking, but the synopsis method, in which you jot down major ideas and concepts in outline form, is probably the easiest and most useful.

What to listen for

1. Listen for a central idea

The central idea of a speech is a statement of what the speaker intends to analyze, prove, refute, or explain. Conventionally, it is stated early in the speech, giving both the speaker and the listeners some guiding notion of what's to come. Without a central idea, a speech will simply leapfrog from topic to topic. Here is an example of a central idea clearly stated in a speech:

> Let me tell you the route I intend to follow in this speech which I probably should have entitled, "The First Amendment, Public Decision Making, and Television." . . . First, I intend to sketch a little theoretical background involving the implications of the First Amendment to the Constitution. Second, I intend to do a flashback and discuss how the political speaker faced the voters in pre-television days. Third, I shall consider how and why television has altered the role of the speaker and the politician.[9]

We have no doubt, from the very outset, what the speaker intends to do.

Listening for the central idea and making a note of it when it's presented will give you a road map of the speech to follow. Irrelevancies, omissions, and points of emphasis are all easier to spot when you know in advance exactly what the speaker is trying to do.

2. Listen for evidence and reasons

Impassioned speakers can rattle off innumerable glib assertions. "Communism is taking over the country"; "Fluoride is poisoning our children"; "UFOs have invaded California"; "Marriage is on the way out." The possibilities for wild generalizations are endless. Nor, for the matter, are specious claims, vague generalizations, and empty platitudes restricted to soap box orators in parks. Eminent speakers may make equally preposterous claims. The conscientious listener who does not wish to be duped by every silver-tongued orator must listen intently for supporting evidence. If none is given, then the speaker's claims should not be believed, no matter how passionately they have been made.

But how does a listener evaluate the validity of evidence? Common sense suggests two simple tests: First, the evidence must be *appropriate* to the claim; second, the evidence must be *confirmable*. If a speaker, for instance, claims that the Soviet Union has surpassed the United States in military might, this contention must be supported by appropriate statistics of relative military strength. Moreover, either the source of the evidence must be identified, or the evidence must be of the kind whose accuracy any interested listener can confirm. If the evidence is irrelevant to the speaker's claims, or if its source is untraceable, then the speaker's claims must not be believed.

Not all evidence, however, is either factual or numerical. Sometimes speakers will support their arguments by citing the opinions of an authority. The validity of *testimonial evidence*—as evidence of this kind is called—depends on the credentials of the authority, and the authority's qualifications to comment as an expert on the speaker's subject. Typically, a speaker will sketch the credentials of an authority before quoting the authority's opinion. Here is an example:

> What I am saying was recently confirmed by a published interview with Alistair Cooke, chief U.S. Correspondent for *The Guardian,* one of England's most distinguished newspapers . . . [followed by Cooke's opinion of American television] [10]

Testimonial evidence is often misused by speakers eager to shout out the opinion of any well-known person sympathetic to their cause. But an authority in one field is not necessarily an authority in another. Alistair Cooke, an authority on the subject of television, may not be an expert on education. Ralph Nader may be an authority on consumer issues, but he is no expert on nuclear engineering. Wary listeners should therefore not only pay careful attention to the credentials of anyone cited as an authority, but should also consider whether the "authority" is, in fact, qualified as an expert on the speaker's subject.

During the course of a speech, speakers are also likely to offer *reasons* in support of their beliefs or in an attempt to sway the audience to their convictions. Sometimes the reasons will be *explicitly* labeled, as when a speaker, explaining the backlash against the women's movement, tells an audience:

> One specific reason for the backlash can be attributed to the identity crisis. Many people see ERA, and indeed the women's movement, in terms of a denial of the differences between men and women. This has been called the interchangeability syndrome.[11]

On the other hand, a speaker's reasons may be *implicitly* embedded in the speech:

> Abortion is often argued for in terms of its beneficiality. It is better, some say, that these young human beings do not come into the world; it is better for them; it is better for the parents; it is better for society at large. And they may be right. It may be more beneficial. But what we are arguing is not beneficiality. We are not arguing pragmatism. We are not arguing convenience. We are arguing right and wrong. It was more convenient for slave holders to maintain a system of slavery, but it was *wrong*. A matter of principle cannot be compromised for a matter of convenience. It cannot be done.[12]

A speaker will often urge the audience to accept a point of view on the grounds that it is morally right or consistent or in some way beneficial; or the speaker may urge the audience to reject a point of view on the grounds that it is morally wrong or inconsistent or in some other way harmful. Frequently there is a link between a proposition which most people accept as valid and the disputed proposition being advanced by the speaker. Anyone who has ever sat through a debate on capital punishment has probably heard arguments like this one: "All human life is sacred. That is one of the cornerstones of our democratic system. It is as close to a self-evident truth as any we subscribe to. And it is because we believe that all human life is sacred that capital punishment—which is the cold and calculated taking of a life by the state—is wrong." Here the speaker is linking a value most people would accept—that human life is sacred—with the proposition being advanced—that capital punishment is wrong.

Most of the great debates of any era involve not so much evidence as they do reasons. Opposition to the Vietnam war, for example, was based largely on the belief that the United States had no right to interfere in the internal affairs of another nation. Debate on the ERA may involve some evidence that women are inadequately protected by existing law, but most of the arguments for or against ERA are based on reasons. Proponents often argue that women deserve equal protection under the Constitution; opponents typically counter that family law should be regulated by the states and not by the federal government. Neither argument is supportable by evidence, since both involve statements of value and belief.

Whether you agree with a speaker's reasons will ultimately depend on your own personal values. Some reasons the speaker gives will be more valid than others; but validity, like beauty, is often in the eye of the beholder. Yet to evaluate a speaker's case it is imperative that you listen to the reasons as well as the evidence given in support of it. (For more on this topic, see Chapter 14, "Persuasion.")

3. Listen for definitions

A *definition* is a statement of what a thing is or of what a word or an expression means. Many of us naively assume that a word means the same thing to everyone who speaks the language. Not only is this often not the case, but it is frequently impossible for antagonistic factions to agree on the meanings even of ordinary words. For instance, during the 1960s, the seemingly innocuous phrase *law and order* had become such a polarizing expression that Richard Nixon, in his speech accepting the nomination for president in 1968, was obliged to say:

> And to those who say that *law and order* is the code word for racism, here is our reply: Our goal is justice—justice for every

> American. If we are to have respect for law in America, we must
> have laws that deserve respect. Just as we cannot have progress
> without order, we cannot have order without progress.

Semanticists divide words into two general groups: concrete
words and abstract words. *Concrete words* stand for physical enti-
ties; abstract words indicate the invisible, the imaginary, the purely
conceptual. *Freedom* has no corporeal form; *love* has smitten many,
but no one has ever seen it. Speakers who use abstract terms are
therefore obliged to define them—especially when such terms have a
special meaning that is crucial to the subject of the speech. In the
following example, a speaker declares that "manners are a sign of
education," and then goes to say what he means by *manners:*

> "Manners are behavior and good breeding," as Addison said,
> but they are more. It is not without significance that the Latin
> language has but a single word [*mores*] both for usage, habits,
> manners, and for morals. Real manners, the manners of a truly
> educated man or woman, are an outward expression of intellec-
> tual and moral conviction. Sham manners are a veneer which
> falls away at the dampening touch of the first selfish suggestion.
> Manners have a moral significance, and find their basis in that
> true and deepest self-respect which is built upon respect for oth-
> ers. An infallible test of character is to be found in one's man-
> ners towards those whom, for one reason or another, the world
> may deem his inferiors. A man's manners towards his equals or
> his superiors are shaped by too many motives to render their
> interpretation easy or certain. Manners do not make the man,
> but manners reveal the man.[13]

The definition goes on in considerable detail, but enough of it has
been quoted here to illustrate its importance in the speech. *Manners,*
as the speaker intends the word, has neither the ordinary nor the
dictionary meaning. The listener who missed this definition could
easily misunderstand an important part of the speech. (Definitions
are also discussed in Chapters 7 and 10.)

4. Listen for appeals

Embedded in the heart of every persuasive speech is an appeal—
an attempt to motivate us to do what the speaker wants us to do or

to believe what the speaker tell us is true. A speaker trying to persuade you to buy an American car instead of a foreign one might
appeal to your self-interest by stating that the fortunes of the American automobile industry affect the nation's entire economy—that, in
a sense, buying the foreign car might eventually cost you your job.
On the other hand, the speaker might urge you to buy American by
insinuating that to do otherwise is unpatriotic. The difference between these two appeals is that the first, at its core, contains a real,
if debatable, issue, while the second is merely emotional.

Later, in the chapter on persuasion, we will consider the legitimate use of emotion in arguments, but for the time being we will
simply note that you should always be suspicious of purely emotional
appeals. The problem with emotional appeals is that they do not lend
themselves to reasonable debate but only to charges and counter-
charges. Appeals to reason, on the other hand, can be answered by
reason—and reason is the forum in which most people would wish
their disputes to be settled. Some arguments, especially those involving deeply held values, may be nearly unresolvable; but arguments
based on reason are always easier to resolve than arguments based
solely on emotion.

5. Listen for recommendations, suggestions, and conclusions

Speakers generally have a distinct purpose in mind. Sometime,
therefore, at the end of the speech, after the speaker has gone over
what is wrong, what is deficient, what is missing, a recommendation
will more than likely be made, a solution proposed, an action suggested, or a conclusion drawn. The listener who misses this stage of
the speech has dined on hors d'oeuvres but missed the entree. Here,
at the conclusion of a speech on the inadequacy of inner-city schools,
a speaker offers her solutions:

> A first step would be to issue federal and state appropriations to
> rebuild and improve schools, to furnish modern technical equip-
> ment and free meals. But no physical change will yield results
> unless there is a concern for the second step. Relevant teacher-
> training programs, classroom textbooks and materials must be
> redesigned with an awareness of inner-city culture. I am not sug-
> gesting that we perpetuate the cultural inadequacies of the in-
> ner-city school, but it is impossible to achieve meaningful,
> productive behavior in an affluent society unless you relate to
> and move forward from the students' own frame of reference.[14]

In many speeches, it is evident long before the end what the speaker intends to propose or recommend. Listeners must nevertheless remain alert or they are likely to miss any unexpected or imaginative solutions that a speaker may offer. Moreover, since this is the stage during which a speaker usually exhorts an audience to action, a listener should be especially wary. You should never leap out of your chair after hearing a speech and rush pell-mell to join the fray. Better, instead, to slowly assimilate and ponder the speech—to ask yourself whether the conclusions are rationally drawn from the evidence; whether the proposed solutions are workable and likely to do any good; and whether the speaker's recommendations provide a reasonable answer to the problem.

Review of applications

Your listening effectiveness can be markedly improved if you get into the habit of actively listening. Our suggestions for improving your listening habits fall into two categories: how to listen and what to listen for. You should prepare yourself by becoming as comfortable as possible and by asking yourself what you know about the speaker and the topic, and by putting aside for the moment any strong opinions or prejudices you might have. Use the lag between the rates of listening and speaking to paraphrase what the speaker is saying and to take notes. During the speech itself, you should listen for the central idea; for the evidence presented; for definitions; for the appeals implicit in the speech; and for the speaker's recommendations, suggestions, and conclusions. You should also evaluate the credentials of any authority whose opinions are cited in support of the speaker's views.

III. CAUTIONS

That listening is not to be taken for granted is the paramount lesson anyone who wishes to be a better listener must learn. *Hearing* may be an unconscious process in which sound waves mechanically strike the eardrum and are automatically recorded by the brain. But *listening* must be worked at with conscious effort. In particular, we must discard the poor listening habits most of us have acquired. Among these bad habits are the following:

1. Don't mentally argue with a speaker

When we hear a speaker arguing in favor of an idea that contradicts our values, our first impulse is to counterattack. But if you're fair, you'll give speakers a chance to present their views before you try to refute them. Suspend your convictions for the duration of the speech and listen to the speaker with an open mind. There are at least two good reasons why you should allow speakers to have their say: It gives you a chance to rethink your views by weighing all the evidence and re-examining all the arguments, and it will give you an opportunity to be reasonably persuaded.

2. Don't lose your temper over words

There are *god* words and *devil* words. *Devil* words, for us, sum up a great wickedness in the world; *god* words represent goodness. To a prude, *pornography* might be a devil word; to the pornographer, the devil word might be *censorship*. *Motherhood* used to be a God word, although nowadays some regard it as a devil word. *Patriotism, free enterprise, freedom* are commonly regarded as god words; *communism, welfare state, socialism* are frequently used as devil words. Your reaction to these words will depend, of course, on what you believe.

The danger is that hearing these words may either goad you into a temper, or lull you into agreement, with the same result in each case—you abandon your critical thinking. You either rage mentally at the speaker or you itch to burst into applause. The aim of effective listening is neither to wildly praise nor to fiercely condemn any speaker, but to critically examine concepts, arguments, and evidence.

3. Do compensate for a speaker's delivery

It is difficult to listen attentively to a speaker whose mannerisms detract from the message. Yet such speakers sometimes present valuable ideas. The trick is to separate the speaker from the speech—to pay attention to the ideas and not to the way the speaker utters them. Admittedly, this is sometimes difficult to do, especially with a speaker who has an annoying tic or who hems and haws or mumbles. Yet the fact is that some great men and women who were notoriously inept speakers were well worth hearing in spite of their delivery defects. A case in point is Oliver Goldsmith, considered one of the most versatile writers of the eighteenth century. Goldsmith was such a bumbling speaker that he inspired this epigram:

Here lies Nolly Goldsmith, for shortness called Noll,
Who wrote like an angel, but talked like poor Poll.

The point is that many speakers who make a good deal of sense may express themselves badly. As an attentive listener, you must compensate for the defects in a speaker's delivery, or, at least, not allow these defects to color your interpretation of the speech.

Review of cautions

Efficient listening must be practiced with conscious effort. You must attempt to rid yourself of bad listening habits. Don't mentally argue with a speaker during the course of the speech; don't lose your temper over *devil* words or be lulled into uncritical acceptance by *god* words; do try to compensate for a speaker's delivery by focusing on what is said rather than how it is said.

NOTES

[1] Andrew D. Wolvin and Carolyn Gwynn Coakley, *Listening Instruction* (Urbana, Ill.: ERIC Clearinghouse on Reading and Communication, 1979).

[2] Wolvin and Coakley.

[3] Wolvin and Coakley.

[4] Ralph G. Nichols and Leonard A. Stevens, *Are You Listening?* (New York: McGraw-Hill, 1957).

[5] According to a survey taken by the Book Manufacturers Institute. Quoted in William Norwood Brigance, *Speech: Its Techniques and Disciplines in a Free Society* (New York: Appleton-Century-Crofts, 1961).

[6] Nichols and Stevens.

[7] Bertrand Russell, "Sidney and Beatrice Webb," In *Portraits* from *Memory* (London: George Allen & Unwin, 1956).

[8] Gauleiter Albert Krebs, quoted in John Toland, *Adolf Hitler,* Vol. 1 (New York: Doubleday, 1976).

[9] Waldo W. Braden, "Has TV Made the Public Speaker Obsolete?" Annual Conference of the American Council for Better Broadcast, Baton Rouge, Louisiana, 25 April 1974.

[10] Braden, "Has TV Made the Public Speaker Obsolete?"

[11] Helen B. Wolfe, "The Backlash Phenomenon: The Equal Rights Amendment," *Vital Speeches of the Day,* 15 August 1976.

12 Ken Lonnquist, "Ghosts," in *Contemporary American Speeches,* ed. by Wil A. Linkugel, R. R. Allen, and Richard L. Johannesen (Dubuque, Ia.: Kendall-Hunt, 1978).

13 Nicholas Murray Butler, "Five Evidences of an Education," address before the Phi Beta Kappa Society of Vassar College, Poughkeepsie, New York, 10 June 1901.

14 Patricia Warren, "Bring Forth the Children," Interstate Oratorical Association Contest, 1971.

FOR FURTHER READING

Barker, Larry L. *Listening Behavior.* Englewood Cliffs, N.J.: Prentice-Hall, 1971.

Geeting, Baxter, and Geeting, Corinne. *Huh? How to Win Through Assertive Listening.* Sacramento, Calif.: Communication Design, 1976.

Weaver, Carl H. *Human Listening.* Indianapolis: Bobbs-Merrill, 1972.

Wolvin, Andrew D., and Coakley, Carolyn Gwynn. *Listening Instruction.* Urbana, Ill.: ERIC Clearinghouse on Reading and Communication, 1979.

Coping with speechfright

I. PRINCIPLES

Speechfright refers to the fear or timidity a speaker experiences before an audience. A majority of us—if we have ever had to speak in public—have at one time or another suffered from it.

We are not alone. Many famous speakers and public personalities have suffered from acute speechfright. Abraham Lincoln used to grimace and shake the first few minutes of every address.[1] Called out of the audience and asked to make a speech while attending the theater, Washington Irving rushed from the building and fled from town.[2] William Jennings Bryan, Mark Twain, Jack Benny, and Ulysses S. Grant all suffered speechfright of varying severity, and Jane Fonda has too. When the *Sunday Times* of London asked 3000 United States citizens to list their principal fears, 41 percent listed speechfright as number 1—above the fear of death (number 6), financial ruin (number 3), and loneliness (number 9).

Symptoms of speechfright

Speechfright, as the second half of the word indicates, is a fear response. Perceiving a threatening situation, the brain mobilizes the body for flight, aggression or attack. Biochemical reactions are set into motion. Adrenalin and thyroxin are released into the bloodstream, speeding up the heartbeat and elevating the blood pressure. The pupils of the eyes dilate; the liver pumps sugar into the blood, increasing available energy. Blood is diverted from the stomach and the intestines and shuttled to the brain and skeletal muscles. Digestion churns to a halt. Respiration speeds up; hairs stand on end, causing a rash of goosepimples. The glandular, vascular, and muscular systems go on alert.

A speaker suffering from speechfright will exhibit any of the following symptoms, either separately or in combination:

Voice:	1.	Quivers
	2.	Too fast
	3.	Too slow
	4.	Monotonous; unemphatic
Verbal fluency:	5.	Stammers; halting
	6.	Awkward pauses
	7.	Hunts for words; speech blocked
Mouth and throat:	8.	Swallows repeatedly
	9.	Clears throat repeatedly
	10.	Breathes heavily
Facial expression:	11.	No eye contact; rolls eyes
	12.	Tense face muscles; grimaces; twitches
	13.	Deadpan expression
Arms and hands:	14.	Rigid and tense
	15.	Fidgets; waves hands about
	16.	Motionless; stiff
Gross body movements:	17.	Sways; paces; shuffles feet[3]

Causes of speechfright

There are several theories about the cause of speechfright. One early study linked speechfright to a trauma the speaker suffered on an earlier occasion while giving a speech.[4] A woman was said to have contracted severe speechfright, for example, because she discovered that her slip was showing while she was addressing a group. Never again was she able to give a speech without reliving the embarrassment of that original incident. But the trauma theory, while it may apply to a few severe cases, cannot account for the innumerable reported cases of speechfright by even experienced public speakers. It is simply too farfetched to believe that so many people have suffered public speaking traumas.

Emotion   Some writers account for speechfright with an explanation that has its roots in the controversial James/Lange theory of emotion—named for the psychologists who advanced it, William James and Carl Lange. Basically, this theory says that emotion results not from physiological activity but from an awareness of emotion. To illustrate this subtle distinction, James cites the case of a man walking in the woods who suddenly encounters a bear. Perceiving the bear as a danger, the man's brain immediately prepares the body for an emergency by putting the muscular, glandular, and vascular systems on alert. According to the James/Lange theory, this instantaneous readiness of the body to cope with the bear is a normal and useful reaction that cannot be regarded as emotion any more than can a cramp in one's belly. What frightens the man is not so much the bear as his awareness of his body's sudden and urgent reactions to it. The man's perceptions that his body had gone into a state of controlled frenzy is therefore the *real emotion.*

This explanation certainly applies to a nervous speaker giving a speech. Half the battle against speechfright would be won if speakers could regard their nervous qualms with the same composure as they view an upset stomach. But this is seldom the case. What often disturbs a speaker most is the uncomfortable awareness of a feeling of utter panic. That awareness is the *real emotion.* Speakers find it especially unnerving to hear the frantic thumping of their own hearts and imagine that their dreadful fear is plainly visible to the audience.

The fact is, however, that a speaker's fear, though acutely felt, is often not visible to an audience. Even experienced speech teachers cannot always tell that a speaker is suffering from speechfright.[5] One study found that the more skillful the presentation of a speaker, the less likely an audience would be to perceive the speaker's nervousness.[6] The implication is that though your heart may be thumping wildly as you give the speech, if you have done your homework and rehearsed the speech diligently, the audience probably won't notice your speechfright.

An increasingly popular view of speechfright asserts that a modicum of nervousness is perfectly normal in any speaker. One researcher put it this way: "To experience nervousness while giving a public speech is normal."[7] Another was more elaborate: " 'Speech anxiety' is not a pathological phenomenon derived from some personality quirk. The student knows, for example, why he is apprehensive; he is fearful, not anxious in an irrational, personality-trait, or pathological sense." [8]

But this sort of explanation is roundabout. To say that speech-fright is normal is merely to say that most speakers suffer from it. Nevertheless, there must be a reason for speechfright. One plausible line of thought suggests that the experience of giving a public speech is frightening because it activates three unwritten fears in our culture—against strangers, staring, and novelty.

Fear of strangers   Most of us grew up being warned by our parents not to speak to strangers. It is a rule we observe from childhood and may eventually pass on to our own children. We chat amiably with a friend in a line at the supermarket, but stand aloof and silent if the line is filled with strangers. It has been recently suggested that this fear of strangers may be learned in early infancy. Laboratory studies reveal that infants up to four months old will readily smile at strangers; inexplicably, this behavior changes dramatically when the infant is six months old. [9] A similar receptivity to strange faces and objects also occurs in very young animals and just as abruptly changes as they grow older. [10] Public speaking, which often involves addressing a group of strangers, no doubt evokes this ancient fear, adding significantly to the speaker's anxiety.

Fear of staring   Staring is universally feared by both humans and animals. Often, a stare is used to signal a threat. Many animals scare off intruders into their territory by staring. [11] In her study of baboons, Jane Goodall found that ambitious male baboons would start a fight for herd dominance by staring at the leader. If the leader returned the stare, the challenge was accepted, and the fight would immediately begin. Goodall also found that any aging, shaky leader who was unsure of his fighting abilities would go to great lengths to avoid meeting a stare, even if the challenger's face was thrust only inches away from his nose, as it often would be. The leader would yawn, close his eyes, look up at the sky, or pretend to be fascinated with some object on the ground. [12]

Giving a speech involves getting up before a crowd of strangers and being stared at. The speaker, unlike an aging baboon leader, cannot go through gyrations to avoid meeting the stares of the audience. Standing on the platform before dozens, even hundreds, of staring eyes, the speaker must casually ignore their stares and go on with the speech. No one can say to what extent this staring contributes to a speaker's feelings of nervousness. But, given the universal fear of staring, a good guess would be that the effect is considerable.

Fear of novelty   Finally, there is fear of novelty—a fear that most of us have experienced at one time or another. Psychologists and writers have recorded instances of it in fact and in fiction. It is a real fear in the animal kingdom and has been observed in ravens, chimpanzees, and rhesus monkeys.[13] Animals encountering objects they have never seen before generally react with panic and threats. Children experience fear of the novel and react to it with varying degrees of curiosity and terror. Most of us can remember vividly the exhilaration—and the fear—we felt over "first-time" experiences— the first time we rode a bicycle, drove a car, went out on a date, or traveled alone. With repetition, of course, these experiences become as familiar and humdrum as anything else we've been doing for years.

Whatever else a speech may be, it is certainly a novel event. Most of us have given few speeches; some of us have never given a speech. When we are asked to make a speech, there is enough novelty in the occasion to cause our hearts to race and our palms to sweat. We must address strangers; be intensely stared at; expose ourselves to a novel situation whose outcome is unsure. Granted, we might be a colossal hit; on the other hand, we might be an ignominious flop. The situation is fraught with uncertainly and peril. We begin to wonder how we will react, whether we will make a fool of ourselves. By the time we mount the podium, we are experiencing the symptoms of speechfright.

Review of principles

Speechfright refers to the fear and nervousness most of us feel when we have to give a speech. Many famous people (including actors and actresses) have also suffered from it. So widespread is speechfright that it was once ranked in a survey of Americans as their number 1 fear. The symptoms of speechfright range from a cracked voice to a tense facial expression. There are many theories about the causes of speechfright. One theory, based on the James/Lange view of emotion, states that speechfright is heightened by an awareness of emotions. Another asserts that speechfright is a normal reaction to the stress of speechmaking. The most likely explanation of speechfright is that it is caused by strong human fears of strangers, staring, and novelty.

II. APPLICATIONS

There is no magical cure for speechfright. If you have to give speeches—and doing so is essential in almost every occupation—you will most likely suffer its symptoms. Your heart may beat a trifle faster; your palms may perspire a little; your knees may quiver and shake a bit. But a little speechfright is not a bad thing. William Cullen Bryant, in his day one of America's best-loved speakers, once said that if the time ever came when he could walk in front of an audience and not suffer speechfright, he would think that he was losing the necessary equipment for giving speeches. Bryant had recognized a paradox of human physiology—namely, that with fear come extraordinary bursts of energy. There are, however, ways to lessen and use speechfright, and the best of these is based on a simple prescription: understand and accept it.

Use your fear energy

We have all heard stories about ordinary people who have scaled ten-foot fences while being chased by a bull; about parents who have lifted impossible weights to rescue their children; about family members who have run into fiery buildings and emerged dragging their unconscious relatives. Adrenalin and thyroxin are generally responsible for these feats. These hormones snap the physiological functions into a peak state of readiness and render the ordinary person capable of amazing feats of strength and energy. Adrenalin and thyroxin also give the speaker the burst of physical energy necessary for effective communication with an audience.

Giving an effective speech requires far more energy and strength than holding a conversation with friends. Impassioned orators have been known to shed ten pounds after one hour at the podium. The bigger the audience, the more of themselves speakers must project. They must concentrate on what they have to say, articulate loudly enough to be heard in the back row, establish eye contact with the audience, emphasize their points with appropriate gestures, and—at the same time—be sensitive to audience feedback. In sum, the speaker must be extraordinarily alert to a degree impossible without the energy provided by adrenalin and thyroxin—the same hormones responsible for the symptoms of fear.

When you deliver a speech, therefore, accept the presence of speechfright as a positive sign that adrenalin and thyroxin are giving you the energy boost necessary to deliver a rousing good speech.

Choose a topic you like

Enthusiasm over a topic can sometimes cause speakers to forget their nervousness. If you've chosen a topic that you're really excited about, chances are that once you begin the speech your speechfright will rapidly fade. Enthusiasm, in any event, tends to be contagious and does help improve the quality of your speech and your contact with the audience, even if it doesn't allay your nervousness.

This rather self-evident prescription seems not to occur to many students, who often grab on to the first convenient and easy topic that comes to mind, regardless of whether it appeals to them. The advice to choose a topic you're enthusiastic about is well worth heeding.

Be prepared

For many students, speechfright is really a thinly disguised fear of ridicule and failure. Nothing protects against failure better than practice. Once you have chosen the topic, gathered the evidence, outlined the speech, and arranged the ideas, the next three steps should be to practice, practice, practice. The point is not to memorize every word of the speech, which would probably result in a wooden and robotlike performance. Instead, practice involves thoroughly understanding the major points of the speech and the sequence in which you intend to make them. It means conducting several "dry runs" through the speech until you're confident about your ideas and your plans to express them.

Focus on a friendly face

Except in the rarest of circumstances, no audience is made up of only hostile faces. There will be at least one (and probably many more than one) face that is friendly and kind. Most people attend speeches because they are sincerely interested in what the speaker has to say. So one way to get over the fear of being stared at by a sea of strangers is to focus on a friendly face in the crowd. Doing so will give you encouragement and moral support when you realize that your words are being receptively listened to by a member of the audience.

Exercise to release tension

Sometimes the interminable waiting for your turn to make a speech can be sheer torture. By quietly exercising as you sit and wait, you may ease your tension and take your mind off the long walk to the podium. You can do isometric exercises—without attracting any attention—by tensing the muscles against each other or against an immovable object. For instance, to exercise the muscles of both arms, place your palms squarely against each other and push as hard as you can. An individual muscle can be quietly exercised by contracting the muscle for a few seconds and then abruptly releasing it.

A good mental exercise to keep your mind off the upcoming speech is active listening. Instead of simply sitting and worrying about how well you'll do when your turn comes, concentrate on the speeches of the other students. Ponder each point; evaluate the supporting evidence; take notes on content; paraphrase the ideas of the speaker. If you concentrate on listening, you're less likely to sit and brood and make your speechfright worse.

Desensitize your speechfright

Desensitizing procedures can be used to rid a speaker of severe speechfright. The idea is to gradually expose a fearful speaker to small increments of the speechmaking process. Once accustomed to one increment, the speaker is exposed to another, until the speechfright is gradually lessened.

If the entire class can be involved in a desensitizing attempt, we suggest the following procedures. (If the entire class will not be involved, you can get together a smaller group of mutually frightened students, find an empty classroom, and follow the recommended program on your own.)

1. Students take turns reading aloud while sitting in their usual places. This step gets students used to talking to the entire class, but spares them the ordeal of having to stand at the lectern and be stared at. Repeat this step until everyone can read freely to the class without feeling panicked.
2. Students take turns standing silently at the lectern. This

step accustoms students to standing in front of the class and being the object of attention. Give everyone a chance to do it comfortably.

3. Students take turns standing before the class and reading something that was never intended to be read aloud—the side panel from a cereal box, a paragraph from a college catalog, the instructions for assembling a bicycle. This step accustoms students to standing before the class and speaking, but spares them the stress of having to improvise. Repeat until each student can do this in a casual and relaxed way.

4. Students take turns standing before the class and reciting any short, memorized passage, preferably a nursery rhyme or a jingle. This step is similar to step 3, except that the student is now reciting from memory, which more closely approximates actual speechmaking. Repeat as often as necessary until every student can perform this step comfortably.

5. Students take turns giving short, prepared summaries of a news story, the plot from a television show, or the main idea of a book. Repeat with different material of gradually increasing length until every student is comfortable doing it.

You will probably find that it is impossible to conduct a program of this sort without a good deal of teasing and laughter from class members. No matter; humor is a good antidote to speechfright. Once the class understands the purpose of the program and begins to associate fun and excitement with speechmaking, its members will be well on their way to overcoming speechfright.

Review of applications

There is no instant cure for speechfright. Most people who give speeches suffer occasionally and briefly from it. One of the benefits of speechfright is that it provides speakers with increased energy and alertness that will actually help them make a better speech. To lessen your speechfright, you should accept and use its fear energy; choose a speech topic you really like; prepare diligently for the speech; focus on a friendly face in the crowd; and exercise to release tension. In cases of severe and persistent speechfright, you can get together with others in your class and conduct a desensitizing program in which everyone is gradually exposed to small increments of the speechmaking process.

III. CAUTIONS

The theme of our few cautions is one commonly applied to the practice of medicine: beware that the cure is not worse than the disease. Students sometimes go too far in trying to allay their nervousness and actually end up giving a worse speech than they would have if they had simply ignored their symptoms of speechfright.

1. Don't write out the speech in advance

The assignment is for you to give a speech, not read a speech. And it's no use thinking that if you're too nervous to give one, you can at least read one. Writing out the speech and then reading it to the audience is an overcompensation for speechfright. You may use an outline and refer to it during the course of the speech; but don't read from a prepared text, no matter how nervous you feel. Doing so will give the speech a literary rather than conversational style and will block the speaker's awareness of audience feedback.

2. Don't give the speech to only one person

Earlier we advised you to focus on a friendly face and draw encouragement from it. Now we caution you not to give your speech *only* to that friendly face. You must also make eye contact with other members of your audience. Obtain encouragement from occasionally looking at one friendly face, but be careful not to ignore everyone else in the room.

3. Don't overprepare the speech

In compensating for speechfright, student speakers sometimes amass such a body of facts and details about the topic that they end up overwhelming the audience. Thorough preparation of the speech is a good defense against speechfright, but you must still be sensitive to the needs and abilities of your audience. It is easy, but not very useful, to tell an audience much more about a topic than it could ever wish to know. Prepare for the speech by gathering more material than you will use; but don't use this excess material simply because it's available.

4. Think of the audience as people rather than a crowd

The attitude of a speaker toward an audience will often either heighten or lessen feelings of speechfright. The speaker who regards an audience as a hostile mob will obviously be petrified of them. On the other hand, the speaker who sees the audience as a gathering of friendly people sincerely interested in the speech is likely to have quite a different attitude about them. Many experienced speakers will therefore try to humanize an audience—to perceive them as kindly and interested people rather than as an anonymous crowd of strangers. It requires only an exercise of the imagination to do and often can lessen your sense of fear.

Review of cautions

In trying to overcome your speechfright, be sure that the cure you adopt is not worse than the disease. Our cautions are therefore mainly warnings against excesses. Don't read from a prepared speech; don't focus excessively on one person; don't overprepare the speech and then overwhelm the audience with a mass of unnecessary detail. And, finally, do try an exercise in positive thinking by visualizing your audience not as a crowd of hostile strangers, but as a gathering of friendly people sincerely interested in hearing your speech.

NOTES

[1] Mildred F. Berry, *History and Criticism of American Public Address* (New York: McGraw-Hill, 1943), p. 847.

[2] Van Wyck Brooks, *The World of Washington Irving* (New York: E. P. Dutton, 1944), p. 36.

[3] Adapted from Anthony A. Mulac and Robert Sherman, "Behaviorial Assessment of Speech Anxiety," *Quarterly Journal of Speech* 60 (April 1974):134–143.

[4] M. L. Goodhue, *The Cure of Stagefright* (Boston: The Four Seas Company, 1927), Chapter 2.

[5] E. C. Buehler, "Progress Report of Survey of Individual Attitudes and Concepts Concerning Elements Which Make for Effective Speaking," report, University of Kansas, 1958.

[6] Anthony A. Mulac and Robert Sherman, "Relationships Among Four Parameters of Speaker Evaluation: Speech Skill, Source Credibility, Subjective Speech Anxiety, and Behavioral Speech Anxiety," *Speech Monographs* 42 (November 1975):302–310.

[7] James C. McCroskey, "Classroom Consequences of Communication Anxiety," *Communication Education* 26 (January 1977):27.

[8] D. Thomas Porter, "Self-Report Scales of Communication Apprehension and Autonomic Arousal: A Test of Construct Validity," paper presented at the Speech Communication Association Convention, New York, November 1973.

[9] Isaac M. Marks, *Fears and Phobias* (New York: Academic Press, 1969), p. 25.

[10] Marks, p. 24.

[11] Marks, p. 30.

[12] Jane Goodall, "Baboon Behavior," lecture given at Beckman Auditorium, California Institute of Technology, Pasadena, 11 December 1974.

[13] Marks, p. 27.

FOR FURTHER READING

Bower, Sharon Anthony. *Painless Public Speaking.* Englewood Cliffs, N.J.: Prentice-Hall, 1981.

Maltz, Maxwell. *Psycho-Cybernetics.* New York: Prentice-Hall, 1960.

McCroskey, James C. "Oral Communication Apprehension: A Summary of Recent Theory and Research." *Human Communication Research* 4 (1977):78–96.

McCroskey, James; Anderson, J.; Richard, V.; and Wheeless, L. "Communication Apprehension of Elementary and Secondary Students and Teachers." *Communication Education* 30 (1981):122–132.

Zimbardo, Philip G. *Shyness: What It is; What to Do About It.* Reading, Mass.: Addison-Wesley, 1978.

Adapting to an audience

I. PRINCIPLES

A speaker is addressing an audience of manufacturers. Her topic is product safety—a subject she deeply believes in. Her purpose is to urge the manufacturers to make safer products. The central idea of her speech is that unsafe products wreak a terrible toll of injury and death on the unwary public, and she has amassed a fearful array of anecdotes and statistics to support this point. Once the audience has heard the horrors she has to tell about unsafe products, she is convinced that they will share her strong views on product safety.

The speech, however, is a flop. The audience is defensive, hostile, and unmoved by the recital of anecdotes and statistics. The manufacturers resent the implication that they are callous about safety. When she concludes, the speaker has a feeling of self-righteousness which comes from a belief that she has made her points without pulling any punches. Yet the sad fact is that not a single point has gotten through.

Consider another scenario. A speaker is addressing an audience of manufacturers. Her topic is product safety—a subject she deeply believes in. Her purpose is to urge the manufacturers to make safer products. The central idea of her speech is that the manufacturer who makes a safe product will earn a higher profit, in the long run, than the one who does not. She has amassed many examples of product liability lawsuits, filed by consumers, that have cost manufacturers millions of dollars in legal fees and liability awards. Her point boils down to this: an ounce of prevention is worth a pound of cure.

This speech is a success. It is listened to intently. The points seem to sink in. There is much agreeable head-nodding and murmuring from the audience during the speech and, afterward, a warm round of applause.

The difference between the two speeches is this: the first speaker prepared her speech without regard for her audience; the second speaker analyzed her audience and crafted a speech to appeal particularly to manufacturers. And although both scenarios are of our own invention, they illustrate an important principle: the message of a speech must be adapted to fit its intended audience or it will probably be ignored or misunderstood.

The idea that a speaker should analyze an intended audience and then adapt the speech to appeal to them is one that most students find a little odd or even somewhat shady. Only on those rare occasions when we intend to manipulate someone do we analyze that person before we actually have a conversation. If, for example, you wanted to wheedle something out of someone, you might think about the best pitch you could use. Any student who has ever gone through the ritual of borrowing the family car has no doubt had to tailor arguments that appealed especially to Mom or to Dad, depending on which of them controls the keys. But for the most part, personal conversations are spur-of-the-moment events that occur without any prior analysis by either participant. That a speech should not be given unless you know to whom you are giving it and why strikes many who are unfamiliar with public speaking as an exercise in deliberate deception.

To understand why this is a mistaken view, you need to be aware of the major parts of a speech. A speech consists of at least three major parts: a purpose, a central idea, and supporting details. The *purpose* of the speech is what the speaker hopes it will accomplish. It is closely allied to the speaker's beliefs. The *central idea* is the main point the speaker is trying to impart; the *supporting details* are those facts, anecdotes, statistics, and data that make the speech clear and believable.

The question then boils down to this: Assuming an ethical speaker, which parts of a speech should audience analysis most affect? The answer: mainly the central idea and the supporting details. Audience analysis should have little or no influence on the speaker's purpose, since ethical communicators do not change their beliefs in order to get through to an audience. But they do present their beliefs in a central idea that will appeal to the intended audience, and choose those supporting details that the particular audience will find most convincing.

In our scenarios of the two speeches given before the manufacturers, both speakers had the same purpose—to urge the manufacturers to make safer products. The first speaker, however, ignored the composition of her audience and chose to bedevil them with horror stories of the carnage unsafe products can cause. The second speaker shaped the central idea of her speech to appeal to the manufacturers—by pointing out the profit benefits of product safety. Neither speaker's essential position was compromised. One speaker was simply more effective than the other.

Review of principles

Speakers should analyze the intended audience of a speech and adapt its message to their particular needs. Yet many beginning speakers find this idea troublesome because it seems to encourage deception. But audience analysis should have little or no influence on a speaker's basic beliefs as they are expressed in the purpose of the speech. Its influence should be mainly in shaping the central idea of the speech, in selecting supporting details, and in the choice of appeals. Honest communicators will analyze an audience not because they wish to deceive but because they wish to communicate.

II. APPLICATIONS

If audience analysis had not been proven useful by a substantial body of research, as it has been, it would still have great merit merely as a matter of common sense. For even the most naive communicator knows that everyone cannot be reached by the same appeals, that explanations which work well on one person or group often fail miserably with another. How, then, should an audience be analyzed? And what should we consider in preparing to speak before a particular audience?

Social psychologists, politicians, and pollsters have spent considerable time and energy trying to fathom the psychology of audiences. The results are sometimes conflicting and frequently inconclusive. Audiences have been classified into types and sorted into identifiable clusters. But while this kind of information may be useful to the professional pollster or politician, the beginning speaker needs merely to know what kinds of questions to ask about an audience and how the answers they produce should affect the speech. Most speakers, as a minimum, will ask the following questions of an audience, and use the answers in the following ways.

How large will the audience be?

Audience size should affect both the content and the form of the speech—both what is said and how it is said. The larger the audience, the greater the chance the speaker may be misunderstood. For larger audiences, a speaker should infuse less personality and offer more specific information and hard data; with a smaller audience, a speaker can be more informal and intimate. Because the chance of being misunderstood is so great, speakers addressing large audiences usually stick to formal, or standard, English—since it is the most universally understood form of the language—while avoiding in-group allusions or regional colloquialisms. With smaller audiences, speakers do not have to be quite as cautious in their phrasing.

What does the audience expect from the speaker?

People become audiences for a reason. Speakers are asked to address audiences because the audience expects something from them. A speaker, then, must find out what the audience wants. Some audiences want to learn more about a topic on which the speaker is an expert; other audiences may merely wish to be entertained. The speaker who understands the needs and expectations of an audience obviously has a better chance of fulfilling them.

What is the average age of the audience?

Knowing the age of an audience is especially useful to a speaker in choosing appropriate examples to include in the speech. An audience made up mostly of people over fifty has lived through the Great Depression and the Second World War, and will vividly remember the assassination of John F. Kennedy. Allusions to these events or examples selected from these historical periods will have a far greater meaning to such an audience than to an audience of college freshmen. Conversely, with an audience of high school students, a reference to some popular television show is more likely to be understood than one made to an episode in the Truman administration.

What is the average educational level of the audience?

Audiences, like individuals, vary in their ability to understand the spoken word. What may seem like a great subtlety to one audience might seem obvious to another. Highly educated audiences generally demand more evidence and are less susceptible to being swayed by emotional appeals. The educational level of an audience should therefore affect the wording of the speech and the examples and allusions used. An educated audience can be addressed in complex sentences and a sophisticated vocabulary; a less educated audience will require the use of simpler language.

What is the occupation of most members of the audience?

Sometimes this question is unanswerable and irrelevant, especially if the audience has come together for a reason unrelated to their work. But where an audience has a common occupation, the speaker can obviously use it as a source of examples. For instance, a speaker addressing a gathering of medical people can use medical references and analogies. By the same token, if the audience consists of English teachers, an allusion to, say, Chaucer, will be instantly understood. All of us appreciate a speaker who speaks "our language"—that is, the language of our particular work or trade. And since audiences are more likely to be persuaded by a speaker they can identify with than by someone they regard as an outsider, it makes sense for a speaker to occasionally use the "trade jargon" of an audience.

An audience's occupation can also tell a speaker what authorities the audience is likely to respect and so affect the speaker's use of testimonial evidence. Different groups esteem different figures as authorities. An audience of trade unionists might be expected to admire the opinions of someone like the late George Meany, for many years president of the AFL–CIO. But an audience of scientists would probably be more impressed by testimonial support from a person like Carl Sagan, the well-known astronomer and writer. The careful speaker will make sure that the audience esteems so-and-so as an authority before asserting that so-and-so supports a claim.

What pastimes does an audience have in common?

This question is also sometimes relevant and sometimes not. If the audience does share a common pastime, then the speaker can draw on it as a source of figures of speech and examples. Knowing an audience's common pastime can also warn a speaker what not to say. For example, the speaker addressing an audience of birdwatchers would know better than to tell stories about dove shooting. Likewise, the audience that shares an interest in dove shooting will care not a whit about bird watching stories.

What does the audience already know about the subject?

A speech must have a beginning, a middle, and an end. But exactly where a speech should begin will depend on what the audience already knows about the subject. For example, the speaker addressing a group of hang-gliding enthusiasts on their sport will be able to skip the basic definitions and get down to more advanced stuff. On the other hand, the same speaker addressing a group that knows nothing about hang-gliding will have to cover the basics of the sport. Finding out what an audience already knows about the subject will enable the speaker to begin at the level necessary to hold the audience's interest.

What common ground do I have with an audience?

If you have listened to a few speeches, you will probably have noticed that speakers often begin by mentioning the similarities they share with an audience. Speakers at an anti-tax rally will typically emphasize that they, too, are taxpayers. Speakers at a meeting of Republicans will make a point of mentioning their long history of Republicanism. Speakers who observe this ritual are obeying a well-known axiom of social psychology and common sense: we tend to like people whom we perceive as similar to us. And, as a general rule, we are more likely to be persuaded by someone we regard as like us than by someone we see as opposed to our way of thinking.

All of us belong to various reference groups—associations we share with others and which frequently influence the way we think. A person may simultaneously be a Catholic, a college student, a consumer, a taxpayer, a Democrat, and a tennis player. Some of these groups obviously promote a stronger sense of identification among their members than others do. Taxpayers may share a nearly universal aversion to increased taxes, yet being a taxpayer cannot affect one's beliefs and attitudes as much as being a Catholic. But in a speech before taxpayers who oppose a tax increase, it is more relevant that the speaker is also a burdened taxpayer—even if he or she may also be a Catholic. On the other hand, in a speech to an audience of Catholics on a topic concerning their faith, the speaker would be better off stressing the shared Catholicism than the fact that everyone in the room also happens to be a taxpayer. The shared association that the speaker will emphasize, in sum, should be the one most likely to influence the audience's acceptance of the speaker's ideas.

Most of you, of course, will not be addressing audiences of birdwatchers, trade unionists, or doctors. As a student, you will be faced with making speeches before your classmates. Yet everything we have said here applies as well to in-class speaking. Every audience, even one consisting of public-speaking students, has a cluster of special characteristics that a speaker can use in planning a speech. One speech class, for instance, may include a majority of business majors; another, a majority of science students. Each will obviously have different interests and will respond to different appeals and topics.

Public-speaking classes are really exercises in simulation training. They give the students real experiences in speechmaking; they duplicate, as closely as possible, the conditions that speakers will encounter in the "real world." Yet there is one basic difference between the speaker addressing an audience of classmates and the one addressing an audience of Rotarians at a dinner—namely, the presence of the teacher in the classroom. Indeed, perplexed students often wonder to whom they should address their speeches—the teacher or their classmates. The answer is—to the classmates. The teacher may be numbered among the general audience—as he or she surely is—but cannot be assumed to be in the majority—he or she surely is not. Granted that the influence of the teacher on the grade of the speech is decisive, yet analysis of a public-speaking class means directing the speech at the majority audience of students, and not merely at the teacher.

Review of applications

The usefulness of audience analysis is supported both by research and by common sense. To analyze an audience, the beginning speaker should ask certain questions: How large will the audience be? What does the audience expect from the speaker? What is the age of its members? What is their educational level? Do most of the members have the same occupation? What pastimes do they share? What do they already know about the subject? And, finally, What common ground do I share with this audience? Answers to these questions will help you frame the speech to appeal to a particular audience by guiding your selection of examples, use of appeals, choice of central idea, and inclusion of supporting detail. This kind of analysis applies as well to classroom audiences you will have to address. The classroom speech must be crafted to appeal to the majority audience of students, not merely to the teacher.

III. CAUTIONS

Our most elementary caution is a warning to play fair with your audience. The cardinal sin of speechmaking—especially persuasive speechmaking—is pandering, and it is one we strongly urge you to avoid. Pandering is the blatant attempt to get on the good side of an audience, even if it means lying about a belief, attitude, or point of view. All speakers are occasionally tempted to feign beliefs they do not have in order to win over an audience. But honest speakers will not lie about their basic views simply to curry favor with an audience. Nor should a speaker feign similarities with an audience that do not exist. Audience analysis means stating your case in the best possible contexts; it does not mean inventing the best possible contexts for your case.

For the classroom speaker, there is one caution that is well worth observing. It has to do with the perils faced by any speaker who must address an audience of similar make-up and background. Since students in a speech class are usually underclassmen of about the same age and range of experience, student speakers who draw too heavily on personal experience or general knowledge often end up telling the audience what they already know. To avoid this, base your speech not only on your personal experience and general knowledge but also on solid research. Start with the assumption that what you already know about the subject is old hat to your audience. Then go to the library and dig for fresh material on the topic.

The flip side of this caution is that you not drastically exceed the audience's capacity for learning. Some speakers have a tendency to get carried away with their subject and to pack their speeches with all kinds of abstruse information. Audiences can only absorb so much technical information—especially in the brief speeches that are usually given by student speakers in the classroom. Rather than trying to cram a mass of technical material into the speech, you're better off focusing on one or two major points and driving them home with solid supporting detail.

So much for the don't's in our cautions. The first positive caution is to take into account the values, attitudes, and beliefs of your audience. It takes no great genius to infer from the composition of an audience the presence of certain values and beliefs about the world. For example, anyone can reasonably deduce that an audience of orthodox Catholics is likely to be unsympathetic to abortion; or that an audience of feminists is very likely to advocate anti–sex discrimination laws; or that an audience of fundamental Christians is likely to hold pro-family beliefs. Nor, for that matter, does a speaker need to plumb the full range of values and beliefs that an audience may hold. What you need to know, more than anything else, is the attitude of the audience toward your subject. Often you can find that out by talking to the program chairman. If your subject is an uncontroversial one, the audience's attitude will most likely be one of benign indifference. But if your topic is controversial, you must learn why an audience believes as they do. Knowing what an audience is likely to think about your subject will also prevent you from making gross blunders: like telling an abortion anecdote to an audience of Catholics; or telling a antibusiness joke to an audience of business executives.

Our final caution is that you follow the advice given earlier and analyze your audience before giving a speech. The easier thing to do—and the approach most students take—is simply to ignore the audience. Such speakers are frequently puzzled by displays of impatience from an audience of business majors listening to a scolding speech about grasping corporations; or from an audience of young Republicans who must sit and listen to a speech in praise of Democrats. Business majors *can* be scolded about grasping corporations; young Republicans *will* listen to praises of Democrats; and manufacturers *can be* lectured about product safety—but only if the speaker has had the foresight to consider the audience and adapt the speech to them.

Review of cautions

Our first caution is to play fair with an audience and not fall to the temptation of currying their favor by feigning beliefs you do not truly hold. Audience analysis means stating your case in the best contexts, not inventing the best contexts for your case. Our second caution is a warning not to base your speeches too heavily on personal experience and general knowledge, since you will probably end up telling the audience what it already knows. Our third caution is to avoid the opposite extreme—namely, swamping the audience with technical information. Our fourth and fifth cautions are *do*'s rather than *don't*'s. Do remember to take into account the values, beliefs, and attitudes of an audience toward your subject. And, above all else, do analyze the audience and make an effort to adapt the speech particularly to them.

FOR FURTHER READING

Bitzer, Lloyd. "The Rhetorical Situation." *Philosophy and Rhetoric* 1 (January 1968):1–14.

Clevenger, Theodore. *Audience Analysis.* Indianapolis: Bobbs-Merrill, 1966.

Holtzman, Paul D. *The Psychology of Speaker's Audiences.* Glenview, Ill.: Scott, Foresman, 1970.

Panderson, Martin; Nichols, E. Ray; and Booth, Herbert W. *The Speaker and His Audience.* 2nd ed. New York: Harper & Row, 1974.

Rokeach, Milton. *Beliefs, Attitudes and Values.* San Francisco: Jossey-Bass, 1968.

SPEECH PREPARATION AND DELIVERY

The topic and the central idea

I. PRINCIPLES

Every speech has a topic and a purpose; this may be said of bad speeches as well as of good ones. The speech must be about something—its topic—and it must be intended to accomplish some end—its purpose. The purpose of the speech may be to urge the audience to some action or to convince them of some belief; the topic may be any one of the infinite variety of things that people talk about. But purpose and topic are the two universals we can expect to find in any good speech.

It cannot be said, though, that all speeches will have a central idea. All speeches *should* have a central idea; all *good* speeches certainly have one. But bad speeches sometimes have no central idea, which may be partly why they are bad, or they may have a central idea that is muddled to the point of uselessness. The first principle of speechmaking, then, is this: a speech must be about something—it must have a topic; and its topic must be summarizable into a single sentence—a central idea.

The central idea

The central idea of a speech—sometimes called the thesis, the specific purpose, or the controlling idea—is an exact statement of what the speech proposes to do. Usually stated early in the speech, the central idea predicts, controls, and obligates the movement of the speech toward a certain direction. Here is an example from a student's speech "Why the White Star liner, the *Titanic*, sank."

> On April 14th, 1912, the White Star liner *Titanic* billed in the newspapers as "unsinkable," struck an iceberg off the coast of Newfoundland and sank with the loss of 1,513 lives. The disaster has inspired poems, songs, sermons, movies, and books. Why did the *Titanic*, a ship thought unsinkable, go down? <u>Two defects in the design of the *Titanic* contributed to the disaster: Her steering was sluggish and unresponsive, even for a ship of her immense size; her traverse bulkheads, which should have made her nearly unsinkable, did not extend all the way up to her deck.</u>

The central idea of the speech—the underlined sentence—promises to answer the question "Why did the *Titanic* go down?" by elaborating on two causes: her unresponsive steering and her badly designed bulkheads.

The central idea of a speech may also take the form of a statement of purpose, as when a speaker announces:

> The purpose of this speech is to explain to students why cafeteria prices have risen so dramatically over the past two semesters.

Or, for that matter, a central idea may be in the form of a question, which the speech then proceeds to answer, as in the following example:

> Why do ships float—have you ever wondered that? The largest passenger liner of all times, The *Queen Elizabeth*, 83,673 gross tons, 1,031 feet long and 118 feet seven inches wide, sailed the seas serenely for years, yet a tiny, 3-ounce pebble tossed into the water will immediately sink. <u>Why should a massive iron ship float, and a tiny pebble sink?</u>

The central idea serves two primary purposes in a speech. First, it restricts the speaker to a specific agenda, thereby discouraging rambling. Once speakers go on record as intending to talk about something specific, there is a good likelihood that they will carry through on their promise without irritating digression. Speakers, on the other hand, who begin speeches with only a vague notion of what they intend to talk about run the risk of endlessly hedge-hopping from one topic to another.

Second, the central idea gives an audience a structure to anticipate, making the speech easier to follow. For instance, the speaker who begins a speech by announcing:

> Two defects in the design of the *Titanic* contributed to the disaster: Her steering was sluggish and unresponsive; her traverse bulkheads, which should have made her nearly unsinkable, did not extend all the way up to her deck.

has informed the audience not only of the main points to be covered but also of their sequence in the speech. The audience expects to hear first about the unresponsive steering of the *Titanic* and then about her poorly designed bulkheads. Anticipating this structure, the audience is better able to follow the speech. In effect, a central idea serves as a focusing device for both speaker and audience, making a speech simpler to give and easier to listen to.

Review of principles

Every speech has a purpose and a topic. Every *good* speech has a purpose, a topic, and a central idea. The central idea may be called the thesis, the specific purpose, or the controlling idea; it has in all cases the same function: to state a specific agenda for the speech. The central idea is a useful focusing device for both speaker and audience. The speaker benefits by knowing exactly what material has to be covered and in what sequence; the audience, by being able to anticipate the direction in which the speech will go.

II. APPLICATIONS

The first thing that a speaker preparing a speech must do is to find a suitable topic. The second thing is to frame this topic into a manageable central idea. Some speech assignments come with tailor-made topics; in that case, the first step has already been done. If the assignment comes with a specific topic, then you can begin by gathering information about it. Many assignments, however, leave topic selection up to the student. What topic you eventually choose will decisively influence the outcome of the speech.

Choosing a topic

Probably the most important advice for beginning speakers is to choose a topic that they truly like. It is obviously easier to talk about something you know and care about, than about something you scarcely know and hardly care about. This is commonsense advice, but it is well worth heeding. If you have to make a speech about a foreign city and have been to London but not to Paris, talk about London. If you loathe English literature but love science, find a science topic for your speech.

But this advice, of course, cannot be pursued to an absurd and selfish extent; some thought should be given to the wishes and tastes of your audience. If the topic you know best and really want to talk about would be remote and alien to your audience, then you must try to find some compromise subject satisfying to you both. Let us say, for example, that a speaker has an overriding passion for ocean liners, and a special love for ships of the White Star Company. Most audiences would probably not be interested in a topic such as "The naval career of the White Star liner *Olympic*"; nor, for that matter, in a talk on "Techniques of traverse bulkhead engineering used in the construction of White Star liners." But an audience might enjoy a speech on "Why the White Star liner *Titanic* sank." Similarly, it is the rare student audience that will willingly suffer through a speech on "Why it is bad strategy in Monopoly to buy utilities"; that same audience, however, would probably be more receptive to a speech on "How Monopoly was invented." The idea is to choose a subject that matches your interest and enthusiasms and, at the same time, takes into account the tastes and temperament of your audience.

Choose a topic suitable to the situation   Sensible speakers pondering the selection of a speech topic should ask themselves these three questions: Why? To whom? and For how long should I speak? The answers to these questions affect the selection of the final topic.

The situation in which student speeches are given is clear-cut and ready-made. As a result, students are tempted to accept it at face value and plod on with the first topic that comes to mind. Resist this temptation. A classroom speech topic needs to be as skillfully chosen as the topic for a speech before the United Nations, if only because students get bored as easily as delegates. Therefore, as you prepare the speech, think about why you are giving it, to whom, and how long it should be.

The "why" is the most readily answered of these questions. Pragmatically, you are giving the speech to satisfy a class requirement. But you must have some more general purpose in mind, or you are sure to ramble. What effect do you wish the speech to have on the audience? Do you want to arouse them to some cause, inform them about some issue, persuade them to some action, or have them laugh so hard they are rolling on the floor? Basically, speeches can be classified under three general categories: to inform, to persuade, or to entertain. These categories are not mutually exclusive. A speaker may inform, persuade, and even entertain in a single speech. But it is useful to conceptualize some general effect that you intend the speech to have, and to bear this in mind not only as you prepare the speech but even before you have chosen the topic.

To whom is the speech to be given? The audience of a classroom speech is curiously dual—made up of many novices and one expert. Your peers in the class make up the novice population; the teacher is the expert. It is, of course, essential that the speech have something in it to please the teacher, who will ultimately grade it. But at the same time, your speech must satisfy your peers, otherwise they will shuffle, cough, mutter to one another, and show other signs of boredom, all of which will no doubt affect the teacher's evaluation of your speech. Bear in mind, before you even jot down the first word or think the first thought, that the topic of your speech has got to satisfy this dual audience.

The final question you should ask yourself is, How long should my speech be? Student speeches are generally restricted to about five minutes, at the end of which time many instructors will promptly interrupt to allow for the next student to give his or her speech. The topic of the speech is necessarily affected by this time limit. Student speeches cannot have long introductions and cannot be interspersed with leisurely asides. The speech must be concise, must move rapidly from point to point, and must pack whatever wallop it has within the space of about five hundred words. A five-minute time limit also means that the topic cannot be complex or broad. Wars and revolutions cannot be covered in five minutes; the evolution of species or the creation of constellations cannot be intelligently discussed in five minutes. Keep in mind, as you select a topic, that five minutes is about the length of time it takes to read aloud a page and a half from a typical book, and that should be the approximate length of your speech.

Finding the central idea

How is the central idea of a speech arrived at? Methods vary from one speaker to another. One speaker might think of the central idea even before researching the topic. Another speaker may be through with the research before a central idea comes to mind. A third may have to pore over masses of information and data before getting the vaguest glimmer of a central idea. Thinking up a speech is not as lock-step a process as, say, baking a cake.

For those students who have trouble devising a central idea, we offer the following two-step method.

Brainstorm on paper   With pen in hand, find a quiet corner and write down the thoughts that come to mind. If your mind is blank, write down "my mind is blank." Work as quickly as you can, jotting down all your ideas, no matter how unrelated. Perhaps, after five minutes of brainstorming, your list might look like this:

1. I hate doing this.

2. My astrological sign is Pisces.

3. I read an interesting book about the *Titanic*.

4. Movies nowadays are very bad.

5. The cafeteria has raised its food prices again.

6. My mind is completely blank.

7. My eye doctor is an optometrist, but my sister goes to an ophthalmologist.

8. I love my mother, but can't stand her sister.

9. My state has adopted no-fault insurance.

10. Libraries are too quiet.

11. Lawyers are overpaid.

12. Mathematics is my worst subject.

Select the best random thought   The preceding list contains several useful ideas for topics. Select the idea that appeals most to you and ask yourself questions about it. For instance, if on item 3 you asked the question "What caused the *Titanic* disaster?" the answer would generate the central idea given earlier. "Two defects in the design of the *Titanic* contributed to the disaster: Her steering was sluggish and unresponsive, even for a ship of her immense size; her traverse bulkheads, which should have made her nearly unsinkable, did not extend all the way up to her deck." On the other hand, the question "Who perished with the *Titanic?*" might produce the following central idea: "The survival list of the *Titanic*'s passengers reveals that a strong class bias was at work in determining which passengers were allowed on lifeboats and which were left to drown." The question asked in item 9, "What is no-fault insurance?" might generate the following central idea: "No-fault insurance is a state law that requires insurance companies to settle personal injury claims of their own clients up to a specific dollar limit without regard to liability or fault." Amplified with appropriate facts, statistics, and examples, this central idea could be the basis for an informative speech about no-fault insurance.

Asking an intelligent question about any of the items on this list doesn't necessarily mean that you'll immediately be able to give an answer. You might have to do considerable research before you can make any sense of the question. Nevertheless, this method of devising a central idea will at least steer you toward a specific and researchable topic.

Review of applications

When you prepare a speech, the first thing you must do is to choose a topic and frame it into a central idea. The topic should appeal both to you and to the audience, should suit the occasion, and should fit into the time allowed for the speech. The central idea is the "angle" on the topic that you will pursue. Finding a usable central idea sometimes requires brainstorming on paper. You select the best random thought that can then be amplified with facts, statistics, and examples.

III. CAUTIONS

Our cautions consist of some specific advice about what kinds of topics to avoid, and what sorts of errors students most commonly make in devising the central ideas of their speeches.

Topics to avoid

Under this general heading fall various topic choices which you should do your utmost to avoid.

Topics that are too technical   If you choose a technical topic for your speech, you are electing to cross the ocean in a leaky boat. You might make it across, but the odds are good that you'll sink before you're halfway there. First of all, technical topics bore the typical audience. Second, technical topics usually require a technical vocabulary, which means that the speech will be riddled with definitions and explanations of the technical terms. Third, technical topics often cannot be adequately explained without charts, graphs, statistics, and illustrations, all of which conspire to do in an audience. Stay away from a technical topic even if it happens to be your pet subject. The following are examples of excessively technical topics:

> The impact of Heisenberg's principle of indeterminacy on subparticle research
>
> Fifty variations on the Sicilian defense in chess
>
> Archetypal criticism of twentieth-century literature
>
> The spinal cord of Hadrosaurus

A topic that in itself is not excessively technical may be too technically treated. Most people, for instance, are aware of astrology and may even read their horoscopes in the daily newspapers. But if you gave a talk on "The meaning of astrological aspects," and spoke about the trines, squares, conjunctions, oppositions, and sextiles in considerable detail, you would probably be telling your listeners much more than they ever wanted to know about astrology.

Topics that are too broad   Vital current issues are very much on our minds; they are discussed on radio and television, and in newspapers, magazines, and books. Most of us are aware of the importance of such issues as the arms race, inflation, and the women's movement. Consequently these are likely to be the first topics to pop into our minds when we have to give a speech. But let's face it, five to seven minutes—the time allowed for the typical in-class speech— is simply not enough time to accommodate a speech on one of these large issues. Moreover, big issues are impossible to research, and difficult to digest. Use your common sense in deciding if a topic is too big. No exact rule exists, but here are some examples of topics that are simply too big to be sensibly covered in a classroom speech:

Discrimination against homosexuals throughout history

Black civil rights movements from Revolutionary days to the 1980s

Feminism in global perspective

Why wars are fought

It is far better to choose a narrower topic that can be adequately covered within the allotted time than to try to subdue a gargantuan topic within the span of five minutes.

Trivial topics   Triviality, like beauty, lies in the eye of the beholder. Some commonsense reflection may be required to avoid the mistake of selecting a topic important to you, but trivial to your audience. For instance, if 99 percent of an audience are men, they will probably regard a topic on "How Hemlines Change" as trivial. Likewise, an audience made up of banking executives is unlikely to regard as important a speech on the topic "How Coupons Can Cut Your Food Bill." Neither audience is likely to be taken with a speech on "What Ever Happened to the Dodo?"—a topic that might be endlessly fascinating to an audience of physical anthropologists. If you are unsure about the importance of your speech topic, poll the class members and ask them about it.

The following are examples of potentially trivial topics:

How frisbees are thrown

Baking a cake at an altitude of 6000 feet

Steps involved in burying a dog

The chemistry of toenail polish

The singing range of parakeets

Intimate topics   Excessive self-confession in a speech is more likely to embarrass than to spellbind an audience. All of us have had intimate experiences and insights that we would love to share. Do so by all means with a friend, a parent, a counselor, a pastor, but not with the audience of your speech class. Personal traumas, tragedies, heartbreaks, and so on, have a limited use as anecdotal asides, but should not be made the principal topic of a speech. Examples of intimate topics that are better left alone are:

My first sexual experience

The greatest heartbreak I have ever suffered

How I almost killed myself

My experience with Jesus

Five errors to avoid in devising a central idea

1. A central idea must not be expressed as a fragment, but must be a complete sentence.

Poor: Cafeteria food prices very high.

Better: The cafeteria food prices have risen dramatically because the wholesale cost of food has gone up and because the new minimum-wage law has doubled the payroll for student helpers.

2. The central idea must not be vague, wishy-washy, or purposeless.

Poor: Bad things happen to your body when you smoke cigarettes.

Better: Cigarette smoking harms the body by constricting the blood vessels, speeding up the heartbeat, clogging the bronchial tubes, and activating excessive gastric secretions in the stomach.

3. The central idea must not contain two unrelated propositions or arguments.

Poor: I favor the Equal Rights Amendment and also believe that people should not be forced to pay into Social Security if they don't want to.

The central idea, as it presently exists, threatens to split the speech into two completely different topics—the Equal Rights Amendment and the fairness of Social Security. One or the other must be settled on, or the speech will tug hopelessly in two directions.

Better: I favor the Equal Rights Amendment because, depending on the interpretation of the courts, it promises to equalize employment opportunities between men and women.

Better: Social Security should be made elective rather than compulsory because it has proved to be a bad investment for many subscribers, and because its solvency is now seriously in doubt.

4. A central idea must not be expressed in figurative language.

Poor: When it comes to poisons, botulism takes the cake.

Better: Botulism poisoning is caused by an anerobe bacillus whose toxin is the deadliest poison in the world.

5. A central idea must not be expressed in muddled language.

Poor: Homosexuality is a statutory offense because the participants are willing so that the relationship is voluntary in character rather than the type described in a victim-perpetrator model.

Better: When participants in a homosexual act are consenting adults, then homosexuality should not be considered a criminal offense.

Review of cautions

Our cautions consist of some specific advice about what topics you should avoid and what errors you should look out for in wording your central ideas. Avoid topics that are too technical, too broad, too trivial, and/or too intimate. A central idea should not be stated as a fragment but rather as a complete sentence; it should not be vaguely expressed; it should not contain two unrelated propositions; it should not be expressed in figurative language; and its language should not be muddled.

EXERCISES

1. Which of the following topics would be suitable for an in-class speech?

   a. The day I got my abortion

   b. Matrilineal kinship affiliation systems among the !Kwong bushmen

   c. How children blow bubbles

d. Famine in the world

e. The impact of cable television

2. Arrange the following topics in descending order from the biggest to the smallest.

a. Marilyn Monroe movies

b. Famous comedy teams in the movies

c. The history of movies

d. The special effects in *Star Wars*

3. Which of the following topics is too technical for an in-class speech?

a. The cause of smog

b. Photochemical reaction of freon on the ozone layer

c. Carcinogens in the water supply

d. Seven steps you can take to avoid cancer

4. Which of the following topics is too trivial?

a. How to give an in-class speech

b. Bathing a canary

c. Why I am an optimist

d. Drug references in pop-music lyrics

5. Which of the following topics is too intimate to be used in an in-class speech?

a. How to buy a used car

b. The usefulness of lovelorn columns in the newspaper

c. What cereal manufacturers put on their labels

d. The guilt I felt when I left my first wife

6. Your speech class is primarily composed of liberal arts majors. Which of the following topics would be the most suitable for such an audience?

a. Buying preferred stock versus municipal bonds

b. The economic theories of Karl Marx

c. The possibilities of hydrogen as a fuel supply

d. Slapstick comedy in modern movies

7. By an enrollment fluke, 95 percent of your speech class is made up of the college's athletes. Which of the following topics do you think is likely to have the most appeal for them?

   a. Shelley as a revolutionary seer

   b. The economic theories of Adolf Hitler

   c. Enlarging your vocabulary through the study of antonyms

   d. Knee injuries in sports: their frequency and cause

8. Criticize the following central ideas.

   a. How life in the ghetto

   b. Woman's liberation is a nutty movement

   c. It was hypothesized that certain physical and demographic data constitute suitable predictor factors in anticipating and evaluating suicide potential among teenagers

9. What is wrong with the following central idea?

   Marie Antoinette was not as bad as everybody makes out plus the guillotine was invented in the eighteenth century as a humanitarian execution method

10. Why would a teacher most likely object to the following central idea?

    Football playing is for the birds

Gathering
materials

I. PRINCIPLES

Every year students utter the same despairing lament, "I can't think of anything to say!" But thinking of something to say is only one of the things you must do as you gather materials for your speech. Of much greater importance is *finding* something to say. And all of us can *find* something to say about anything if we look long and hard enough.

Ideally, your search for materials to use in your speech should be guided by the three principal parts of every speechmaking event: the speaker, the topic, and the audience. Everything you look for, find, and use should bear some relationship to one or the other of these.

The speaker

The first—the speaker—is the most obvious, yet least reliable, source for material. All of us have had a variety of personal experiences, and most of us make the mistake of placing an exaggerated value on them. Beginning speakers often believe that all they have to do is get up and talk about the topic they know best. For instance, students reared on turkey farms might consider themselves expert enough to make a speech about turkeys without doing any preparation; likewise, students who grew up around sailboats might think they could give an unresearched speech about sailing.

No doubt some of us have had rare experiences that could make up the greater part of a speech. But personal experience is just as likely to involve a *narrow* as a *representative* view of a topic. The student, for example, who has spent a lifetime around small center-board sailboats is no expert on blue-water sloops. And while experience with small coastal sailboats can furnish a speaker with interesting anecdotes, it probably won't be enough on which to base an entire speech on sailing. In short, your own experience can be a valuable source of material so long as it is not the only source.

The topic

The choice of an appropriate topic can also guide your search for materials. All speeches are subject to limitations of time and place. Student speakers are usually allowed five minutes to speak. A five-minute speech cannot be twenty pages long. It cannot be about wars and civilizations. If you begin to dig into your topic and find yourself sifting through a staggering amount of information, your topic is probably too big. Now is the time—while you are searching for materials—to find that out, not when you're actually standing before the audience.

Some topics are also naturally better suited to some places than are others. It will probably be easier to gather material on the causes of smog if you live in a city like Los Angeles, where the word has a vivid meaning, than in a rural area, where the air is always clean. Likewise, if your school is in an agricultural region, there will probably be more local experts to consult on a farming topic than if it is sandwiched between the concrete catacombs of a city. This is not to say, however, that you should never choose a topic unless it is somehow relevant to your community. It is merely to remind you that, when you are choosing a topic, you should take into account the availability of materials and the ease with which they may be gathered.

The audience

The audience should also have some bearing on your search for materials. As we stressed in Chapters 4 and 5, intelligent speakers adapt their speeches to their audiences. Assuming that you have chosen a suitable topic, you need to know at what level you should begin your speech, approximately what kind of material you should cover, and what sorts of supporting detail you should include. These choices should be dictated by a knowledge of your audience. For example, if you were giving a speech on the causes of smog to a class in Los Angeles, you know that you can skip a lengthy description of smog. Or if you are giving a speech on a farming topic at a school in a farming region, you can reasonably assume that your audience already has a general knowledge about the topic. Knowledge of your audience can tell you what kinds of materials you need; knowing what kind of materials you need can tell you where to look.

Types of materials to look for

Basically, what kind of materials are you going to look for? The answer is that you are after a mix of information and examples. Facts and numbers tell the speaker's story in an objective way. Anecdotes and lively examples humanize the story and drive it home. In a speech about unemployment in your hometown, for example, you would need statistics to paint the overall picture. But you could make your speech more graphic by giving testimonial evidence from a laid-off worker who can personally describe the frustrations of being without a job. (Anecdotes are discussed on pages 89–90.)

Few student speeches will contain the judicious blend of material that we recommend. Most students, on hearing that they have a speech to prepare, will simply begin digging in the library for facts. No doubt the library is the best place to look for facts. But you should also remember that in your own community there may be people who can bear vivid and graphic testimony to what all those facts mean.

Review of principles

Your search for materials should be guided by the three principal parts of any speechmaking event: the speaker, the topic, and the audience. As a speaker, your personal experiences can be a source of knowledge and anecdotes, but personal experience should seldom be the only source. The choice of topic can make it hard or easy to find the materials you need. A topic that has some bearing on the local community may be easier to research, since local experts are more likely to be available for interview. A knowledge of your audience should tell you not only what kinds of materials you'll need but also where you'll have to look. Your aim should be to find a combination of information (facts and figures) and anecdotes so that you can give the broad objective picture while portraying it in human terms.

II. APPLICATIONS

You have a topic; you know your audience; you understand the limitations of time and place your speech will be subjected to. Now you have to gather materials on your topic. How can you do this systematically?

Take a self-inventory on the topic

A self-inventory means sitting down and systematically asking yourself questions about your speech topic. Why did you choose this topic? Where did you first encounter it? What is your attitude toward it? What do you really know about it? What experiences have you had with it? Do you know anyone else who's had experiences with it?

The self-inventory is intended to dredge up any information you have on the topic that can be used in the speech. Most of the time the self-inventory will produce anecdotal material, examples from real life, or personal observations. But it may also give you a slant on the topic by telling you what really appeals to you about it.

The self-inventory should be conducted on paper. When you have finished, you should have some material that you could use, as well as a general idea of your own knowledge or ignorance of the topic. Knowing how much (or how little) you know about a topic can give you an idea of how much time you'll have to budget for researching it.

Take an inventory of your audience

Your aim in gathering material is to assemble it into a speech for a specific audience. There's no point in boning up on what's likely to be obvious to your audience while ignoring what they really need to know. The audience inventory can tell you what you need to research, and what you don't.

There are various ways to conduct an audience inventory. If your class is small, you can simply talk to most of its members and ask them what they know or how they feel about your topic. If your class is large, it might be easier to use a questionnaire.

Basically, you should ask questions that will tell you what your audience already knows about the topic, and what it might need to know. You can either allow the students to answer in their own words—in which case the results will be more difficult to interpret because of the varied answers you are likely to get—or you can ask them to choose one of several preprinted answers. For example, if you intended to give a speech about word processors, you could ask on your questionnaire, "What do you know about word processors?" and either leave a blank space for an answer, or include three or four possible choices, such as "Nothing; A little; A lot." The best thing to do, before you draft the questionnaire, is to ask yourself exactly what you want to know. Then word each question so that it will yield that information.

Talk to people about your topic

People can be a source of useful information. In nearly all communities there are a surprising number of experts available, and most of them are more accessible that you might think. In any given community, too, there are people who can round out your statistical picture with anecdotes and examples from their own lives. Some of these will be obvious and easy to find. For example, if you were giving a speech about earthquakes, you know right off that a trip to the geology department will put you in a nest of experts.

But some of the experts available for interview may not be so obvious. In a free economy such as our own, salespeople are often an indispensable source of information. If you were giving a speech about word processors, you could call up and arrange to interview some of the word processing salespeople with local computer companies. Most salespeople are willing to talk about their products to students even if there is no chance of an immediate sale. Just make it clear from the outset that you are giving a speech and wish to learn more about their product. Don't try to masquerade as a prospect unless you really are one.

Indeed, most businesses, and most government agencies, are usually in hot pursuit of any favorable publicity they can get. Almost all large firms have public relations departments which exist to make information available about them and their products. Most of the time a phone call to the public relations department will put you in contact with an informative representative who can add substantially to your speech.

And then, too, there is the individual—sometimes cast in the role of a testifying sufferer, sometimes as a live witness to what you are talking about. Consider, for example, a speech on the effects of a drought in your state. You can talk to state officials who will be more than willing to give you the arid numbers. But your speech will need more: it will need the voice of the little man or woman who can give a firsthand idea of how drought affects a farmer. So after you've gotten the overall picture from officialdom of how bad the drought is, get on the phone and arrange to interview one or two real farmers who can give the human side of the story.

Of course, sometimes it isn't possible to meet an expert or witness face to face, in which case we suggest that you write a letter or use the telephone. That more students do not use the telephone in their research, and that most never even consider writing a letter, is something of a mystery to most teachers. A letter from a distant expert written in reply to your query can be an impressive source. Short interviews on your topic can be conducted over the telephone. Information that is sometimes unavailable in one community can often be found in another. One student who was preparing a speech on word processors found the local word processor vendor in her community unwilling to cooperate. So she waited until the cheapest dialing period and phoned the West Coast dealer for the same company. This time she got hold of someone helpful, who gave her all the information she wanted—and more.

Interviewing

But let us assume that you have access to local experts and you make arrangements to talk to them. To talk to people about your topic, you have to interview them. The interview is a talk with a purpose. It is not merely like sitting down with a friend and swapping opinions. You begin by knowing what you want to get out of the conversation; you ask questions that elicit the information you want.

The kinds of questions an interviewer may ask are classified according to the sorts of answers they are likely to evoke. An *open question* requires an interviewee to respond with an opinion or a statement. For example, if you asked a farmer, "What effect has the drought had on your farm?" you are asking an open question. The farmer cannot answer it reasonably in one word, but must supply the details you want.

In contrast, the *closed question* can be answered in one word and is therefore not likely to produce the kind of information you want. For example, if you asked the same farmer, "Do you think the drought has been as bad as everyone says?" you could get a useless answer of "yes" or "no." Open questions are generally better than closed questions simply because they encourage more complete answers.

The *summary question* restates what the interviewee has said while moving the interview on. For example, you might ask someone, "Since you say that you object strongly to the government's handling of inflation, what program would you like to see put into effect?" The first half of the question sums up the interviewee's objections; the second half asks for an opinion of what else can be done.

Conducting a useful interview is largely a matter of social common sense. You should not goad your interviewees, unfairly represent their views, or try to corner them with hostile questioning. You should make encouraging responses whenever you can, either by nodding or murmuring to signify your attentiveness. People usually talk freely to someone who seems genuinely interested in their opinions. You should also make it clear from the outset, after you have exchanged preliminary pleasantries, what you expect to get from the interview. Don't be shy about announcing your topic or making it clear what information you're after. Structure and purpose, after all, are what distinguish the interview from the casual chat.

Using the library

The library is the principal source of information and the place to which all researchers must eventually go. Information stored in the library is contained in books, newspapers, magazines, journals, microforms, and other materials. To do research in the library, therefore, you need to understand the systems that libraries use for retrieving stored information and data.

The card catalog

Basic research begins with a search of the card catalog, which literally puts a wealth of information at your fingertips. The card catalog is an alphabetical index of all the books and periodicals in the library. Consisting of 3-x-5-inch cards that are stored in drawers, the catalog lists each book under at least three different headings, with a separate card for each heading: author, title, and subject. A book that straddles two or more subjects will be listed separately under each subject. If an editor, translator, or illustrator is involved, the book will also be listed under the name of each, in addition to its listing under the name of the author. A book with more than one author is also likely to be listed under the name of each author.

Classification of books

Books are filed either under the Dewey Decimal system or the Library of Congress system and stored on shelves called *stacks*. Large libraries often do not allow students to wander in the stacks. Instead, admission is restricted to library employees who will fetch any requested title. Most libraries put out a flyer that explains the classification system used. If you do not understand the system, ask your librarian for help.

Classification of periodicals

Periodicals and newspapers are classified differently from books. Current issues are usually shelved alphabetically by title and are accessible to the public. Back issues, either bound in book form or reproduced on microfilm, are stored elsewhere—usually in a special section of the library. Depending on whether the stacks are open or closed, the public may or may not be admitted.

Classification of nonbooks

Nonbook materials—films, microfilms, recordings, newsclippings, sheet music, reproductions of works of art, transparencies, slides, programmed books, and other similar materials may be listed either in the general catalog or as a special collection. No hard-and-fast rule exists for classifying this kind of material, so you must ask your library staff which method the library uses.

The references

The reference section is the nerve center of the library. Reference books systematically list and sum up the information to be found on specific topics. The experienced researcher, therefore, usually begins a search for information by consulting first the card catalog and then the general references.

General references index information available on a variety of subjects; specialized references index information on specific subjects. Listed on the following pages are the best-known general references.

Books listing other books

Publishers' Trade List Annual. New York: Bowker, 1873–present. Includes publishers' catalogs, alphabetically arranged. Two important indexes accompany this book: *Books in Print: An Author-Title Series Index* and *Subject Guide to Books in Print: A Subject Index.* Both indexes are published annually. Useful for checking if a book is still on the market.

Paperbound Books in Print. New York: Bowker, 1960– present. Monthly record of paperback books. Contains a cumulative index. Listed here are all paperbacks in print.

Books listing book reviews   Books that list book reviews are useful guides whose entries frequently synopsize information about a reviewed book. If you want, for instance, to get the gist of a certain book but don't want to go to the trouble of reading it, check the *Book Review Index* and read what the reviewer had to say about the book.

Book Review Digest. New York: Wilson, 1905–present. Lists reviews from all major American and English periodicals. Published monthly except February and July, with annual cumulations.

Book Review Index. Detroit, Michigan: Gale Research Co., 1965–68, 1972–present. Lists reviews appearing in all periodicals of general circulation.

Indexes of periodicals and newspapers   These indexes alphabetically list topics of magazine and newspaper articles, giving the name of magazine or newspaper in which the article occurred and page number.

Poole's Index to Periodical Literature. 1802–1907. 7 vols. Boston, Mass.: Houghton Mifflin, 1882–1907. This pioneer work indexes close to 600,000 articles in American and English periodicals. Contains a subject index only.

Readers' Guide to Periodical Literature. 1900–present. New York: Wilson, 1905–present. Published semi-monthly (monthly in July and August) with quarterly and annual cumulations, this is by far the most popular periodical index, and has been widely used to research sources for thousands of undergraduate and graduate papers and speeches. Contains an author, subject, and title index to about 160 notable magazines in various fields.

Social Sciences and Humanities Index. New York: Wilson, 1965–present. Replaced *International Index.* New York: Wilson, 1907–1965. Since 1974, published separately as *Social Science Index* and *Humanities Index.* An excellent guide to essays in scholarly journals such as the *New England Quarterly* or *Political Science Quarterly.* Includes a subject and author index.

New York Times Index. New York: The Times, 1913–present. A semimonthly and annual index to the daily issues of *The New York Times.*

Index to the Times. 1906–present. London: Times, 1907–present. A thorough bimonthly index to the *London Times.*

Newspaper Index. Wooster, Ohio: Newspaper Indexing Center, Bell and Howell, 1972–present. Indexes articles appearing in the following newspapers: *Chicago Tribune, Los Angeles Times, New Orleans Times-Picayune,* and *Washington Post.* Includes subject and author indexes.

General knowledge books: encyclopedias   The encyclopedia is the czar of general knowledge books and a good place to begin research on almost any topic. The *Encyclopaedia Britannica,* by far the best encyclopedia available, contains useful articles on a vast array of topics. Your library will no doubt have at least one or two encyclopedias on hand, and we recommend that you consult them for information on your topic.

Books about words: general and specialized dictionaries   A dictionary provides information about the meaning, derivation, spelling, syllabication, linguistic study, and usage of words. It also gives synonyms, antonyms, rhymes, slang, colloquialisms, and dialect. Specialized dictionaries exist that similarly classify and explain taboo words, slang, and colloquial expressions and phrases. Dictionaries are useful sources of definitions. Consult your librarian for information on the various dictionaries available in your library.

Books about places: atlases and gazetteers   For information about places, consult any of the various atlases or gazetteers available in your library. Atlases generally contain useful maps, charts, tables, and plates that provide information about the people, culture, and economy of countries. A gazetteer is a geographical dictionary or index that gives basic information about the most important regions, cities, and natural features of the countries of the world. Researchers consult gazetteers when they want information about the legal and political status of a country, its location, and important features. Consult your librarian for information on the gazetteers available in your library.

Books about people   Numerous biographical sources are available on persons both living and dead. *The International Who's Who* provides sketches of living persons all over the world. Moreover, there are *Who's Who* volumes that list notables by both country and profession such as *Who's Who In Australia* and *Who's Who In American Politics*. For further information on the *Who's Who* volumes or on any of the various biographical dictionaries available in your library, ask the librarian.

Books about government publications   For information about government publications, ask your librarian to direct you to the various available indexes to government publications. The following are especially useful:

> U.S. Superintendent of Documents. *Monthly Catalog of United States Government Publications.* Washington, D.C.: Government Printing Office, 1895–present. A monthly catalog, arranged by departments, that provides up-to-date listings of publications from all governmental agencies. Includes subject indexes.

> U.S. Superintendent of Documents. *Checklist of United States Public Documents, 1789–1909.* 3rd ed. Washington, D.C.: Government Printing Office, 1911. Covers 120 years of government printing.

> U.S. Superintendent of Documents. *Catalog of the Public Documents of Congress and of all Departments of the Government of the United States for the Period March 4, 1893, to December 31, 1940.* 25 vols. Washington, D.C.: Government Printing Office, 1896–1945. A comprehensive summary of government materials published before 1941.

Various commercially produced guides and indexes to government publications are also available. Ask your librarian.

There are also reference books that classify information and data available on specific subjects. Depending on the complexity of your topic, a specialized reference may or may not have to be consulted. Check with your librarian about any special problems you might be having in finding material on your chosen subject.

Using ERIC: computer-assisted research

ERIC is the acronym for the Educational Resource Information Center. Basically, ERIC is a nationwide system of clearinghouses that gather, coordinate, index, and catalog locally produced and unpublished materials such as project reports, speech texts, research findings, and conference reports. The sixteen ERIC clearinghouses specialize in one of the following subjects: career education; counseling and personnel services; early childhood education; educational management; handicapped and gifted children; higher education; information resources; junior colleges; languages and linguistics; reading and communication skills; rural education and small schools; science, mathematics, and environmental education; social studies and social science education; teacher education; tests, measurement, and evaluation; and urban education.

Two kinds of searches are possible under the ERIC system: a manually operated search of the ERIC references and indexes, and a computer assisted search. ERIC has indexes that catalog and classify information on one hundred thousand documents. Moreover, this information is also stored on magnetic tape for computer retrieval. In sum, if your speech topic falls under one of ERIC subject areas, it is possible that the computer in your college library may be used to help you in your research. Ask your librarian.

Review of applications

The first step in gathering materials is to take a self-inventory of what you already know about the topic. A self-inventory will often produce anecdotal material or examples; it will also give you an idea of how much time you'll need to do your research. The second step is to inventory your audience, finding out what kinds of material is most likely to appeal to them and what they already know about the topic. Both inventories will give you a useful idea of what kinds of material you need to look for. Interviewing local experts and witnesses who can be sources of information is the third step. Experts of every kind can be found is almost every community, and most of them are more accessible than you think. The most obvious place to look for materials is the library, where information is available in books and periodicals, on microform, and in other materials. ERIC—computer-assisted research of locally produced and unpublished materials—is also available in many large libraries and can help you locate material not otherwise cataloged.

III. CAUTIONS

The first and possibly the most necessary caution is not to build your speech around a single source of material. Do not assume, as many students do, that your own experience with a topic is enough for any speech. Most of the time it isn't. Many potentially good speeches have suffered because the speaker mistook narrow personal experience for the last word on a topic.

In line with this caution, we also urge you not to rely too heavily on only one kind of data. Speeches crammed with facts and statistics but entirely lacking in anecdotes and examples are hard to listen to. Tell your audience the somber statistics about topsoil loss on Midwestern farms; then relate the case of Farmer Brown, whose wheatfields have all but blown away.

We also caution you to search specifically for material that will appeal to your audience. Adapting a speech to an audience should not take place *after* the material is all gathered and outlining begun. It should, in fact, begin *before* you have even started to search for material. Indeed, a speech needs to be adapted in both form and content—in both what you say and how you say it. This important point should guide the direction of your research.

Bear in mind as you do your research, moreover, that you should be looking for visual as well as written material (see Chapter 7). Some speeches are better suited to the use of charts and graphs, especially if the topic is technical or otherwise difficult. On the other hand, if your topic is simple enough not to require illustrations, by all means leave them out.

Finally, remember that the materials you gather are a means to an end and not an end in themselves. Every diligent researcher will end up with more material than is needed in the speech. Material that cost a day's digging might have to be discarded if it turns out to be either irrelevant or unnecessary. Your aim in gathering material is to support the points you intend to make in your speech. If you cannot use the material, don't be afraid to omit it. Better to do that than to cram every ounce of data into your speech and end up boring the audience.

Review of cautions

The speech should not be based on a single source of materials, but should draw material from many different sources. It should paint the objective picture while investing it with human appeal. Your search should be geared to the needs of your particular audience. If your topic is technical or otherwise difficult, you should also look for charts and other graphics that will help illustrate your point. Finally, you should not be reluctant to discard unnecessary or irrelevant data, no matter how much effort such material took to find.

How to use
supporting details

I. PRINCIPLES

"A speech has two parts. You must state your thesis, and you must prove it." This observation of Aristotle's is over 2000 years old but just as applicable to speeches today as to those made in ancient Greece. Most speeches do consist of two parts: a central idea and supporting details. The central idea is the principal point the speaker is trying to impart (see Chapter 5). The supporting details are those facts, data, and other kinds of evidence that prove it.

Consider this example. A student is giving an in-class speech against the hot dog. Simply stated, the central idea of her speech is that hot dogs are nutritionally worthless. She has done what she thinks is adequate research, assembled her findings into an outline, and is now ready to make the speech. Below is a paragraph from the speech as it was delivered.

> Hot dogs are bad for you. They can make you feel sick. They have a lot of fat and little protein. Many authorities in the field of consumer protection have declared that hot dogs have no nutritional value. They contain a blend of artificial additives and chemicals that have a negative effect on the human physiology. In fact, under the FDA, the quality of hot dogs has gotten worse,

because hot dog manufacturers are now allowed to put all kinds of foreign substances and fillers in hot dogs, things that aren't good for you. You can get fat from them, while starving your body of badly needed nutrients.

The student went on for another three or four minutes in more or less the same vein, finally concluding with a weak plea that the audience refrain from eating hot dogs. The result of all her persuasions? A politely uninterested audience and a rather poor grade. The instructor stated in an evaluation that the speech was too general and that the student failed to make a specific and substantial enough case against the hot dog.

This student speech suffered from a defect common to many everyday assertions and arguments: excessive vagueness. Everything the student had said was indeed true, and she made no assertion that she hadn't either read or heard somewhere. Her audience, no doubt, had also heard and read something similar about hot dogs. But by failing to support her claims and arguments with specific details, she persuaded no one and communicated little of value.

Specific details

An assertion may be generalized or it may be made in specific detail. Because it is easier to rattle off generalizations than to talk in specifics, all of us at one time or another are guilty of blithely generalizing: "Coffee is bad for you"; "Inflation is very high"; "Football players are dumb"; "Blondes have more fun"; "Communists are horrid." The catalog of generalizations that you can hear in the everyday world is endless. And while it may be unreasonable to expect casual conversation to be rigorous and exacting, it is certainly not unreasonable for an instructor to expect the assertions of an in-class speech to be made in a specific detail. To illustrate how the same assertions can be made in varying degrees of specificity, we have prepared a chart listing alternatives to many of the student's assertions about the hot dog:

I	II	III
Vague	*Less Vague*	*Specific*
Hot dogs can make you feel sick.	Hot dogs can give you headaches.	Hot dogs are cured with sodium nitrate, a substance which, according to the American Academy

I *Vague*	II *Less Vague*	III *Specific*
		of Neurology, causes headaches in many people.
Hot dogs have a lot of fat and little protein in them.	*Hot dogs have about 10 percent protein and 90 percent fat and other substances.*	*The U.S. Department of Agriculture claims that today's hot dogs are comprised of 29 percent fat, 11.7 percent protein, and 60.3 percent salt, spices, preservatives, and water.*
Many authorities in the fields of consumer protection have declared that the hot dog has no nutritional value.	*Ralph Nader and other consumer rights advocates agree that hot dogs are nutritionally worthless.*	*"Hot dogs," says Ralph Nader, "are among America's deadliest missiles"; a former Consumer Affairs Commissioner for New York City, Bess Myerson, agreed: "After I found out what was in hot dogs," she said, "I stopped eating them."*

The assertions made in any speech should be supported by the sort of specific details found in column III. Generalizations, of course, have their place; one cannot give a speech filled entirely with details without becoming excessively technical and boring. But whenever an idea is presented that is crucial to the central contention of your speech, you should support it with as many details as you can possibly muster.

Review of principles

Speeches generally consist of two parts: a central idea and supporting details. The central idea is the main point of the speech; the supporting details are those assertions that back it up. In making a speech, you should support your ideas with as many specific details as necessary to convince your audience.

II. APPLICATIONS

The various kinds of details that can be advanced in support of any idea or claim include facts, definitions, examples, testimonials, statistics, anecdotes, and diagrams.

Facts

A fact is an assertion about reality. The assertion is a fact (1) if it accurately represents reality and (2) if it is verifiable. The first condition simply says that to be a fact, an assertion about something must be true; the second condition demands that this truth be the same for any two people.

Consider, for instance, the following assertion about the Shroud of Turin. "The material of the cloth is linen, handwoven in a herringbone twill—a pattern known to the ancients. It was found to contain pollen grains from plants common in areas around the Dead Sea and Palestine." This statement qualifies as a fact because it is both true and verifiable. The Shroud of Turin does consist of linen woven in a herringbone twill, and fabric patterns of this type do date back to the days of Christ. The presence of pollen grains on the fabric traceable to plants common around the Dead Sea and Palestine was reported in published research by the Swiss criminologist Max Frei. On the other hand, a statement such as "Astrological forces influence the performance of the stock market" must be regarded as a statement of belief rather than as an assertion of fact, since the effects of astrology have never been adequately demonstrated.

Facts add a convincing ring to any speech. The speaker who makes a vague assertion such as "In 1978, many scientists studied the Shroud of Turin for many hours and conducted many sophisticated tests on it" sounds uncertain and a little fuzzy. Better, and far more convincing, to do the legwork necessary to allow you to more specifically describe the tests that were done: "In 1978, twenty-four scientists were given permission by the Catholic church to study the Shroud. They examined it for 120 hours using seventy-two crates of electronic gear. They took eight photomosaics of it; processed sixty pairs of X-ray film; and recorded thirty-six X-ray-fluorescence spectra, eighty-five infrared scans, and eighteen thermograms. Thirty-two samples were lifted off the linen with sticky tape."

Sources for facts   The reference section of a library is the best source of facts available to the student speaker. Encyclopedias found there provide excellent summaries of state-of-the-art facts on a variety of subjects. Reference volumes of various kinds, including the indexes and abstracts on different subjects, are also prime sources for facts. (See Chapter 6.)

Definitions

A definition is a statement of what a thing is or of what a term or concept means. Experienced speakers, who give speeches on complex topics, usually begin by defining all crucial abstract terms. Here, for example, in a speech entitled "Why I Am an Agnostic," delivered at a religious symposium in 1929, the famed trial lawyer Clarence Darrow begins by saying what he means by *agnostic;*

> An agnostic is a doubter. The word is generally applied to those who doubt the verity of accepted religious creeds of faith. Everyone is an agnostic as to the beliefs and creeds they do not accept. Catholics are agnostic to the Protestant creeds, and the Protestants are agnostic to the Catholic creed. Anyone who thinks is an agnostic about something, otherwise he must believe that he is possessed of all knowledge. And the proper place for such a person is in the madhouse or the home for the feeble-minded. In a popular way, in the western world, an agnostic is one who doubts or disbelieves the main tenets of the Christian faith.[1]

Because abstract terms symbolize ideas, notions, or concepts that can be variously interpreted by different listeners, it is especially necessary for speakers to define all such terms in the speech. The student giving a speech on a topic such as "The Role of Love in Modern Marriages" should begin by defining *love*, since it is a term fuzzy and abstract enough to trigger off many contradictory interpretations in an audience. (For a full discussion of *abstract* and *concrete* terms, see Chapter 10.)

Sources for definitions   An obvious and useful source for definitions of terms is the dictionary, in all its various forms. Some dictionaries define the formal words of standard English; others catalog the origins of various slang terms.

Examples

Examples can provide a listener with a specific application of a general idea or principle. Without examples, assertions tend to sound vague and unconvincing; illustrated with adequate examples, even the most farfetched assertion sounds probable. Here is an example:

> Jonah could have been swallowed whole by a sperm whale. . . . A ship in the South Seas in 1771 had one of her boats bitten in two by a sperm whale. The beast seized one unlucky crew member in her mouth and went down with him. On returning to the surface the whale ejected him on the wreckage of the broken boat, much bruised but not seriously injured. . . . A worse fate befell another victim in 1891. The *Star of the East* was in the vicinity of the Falkland Islands and the lookout sighted a large sperm whale three miles away. Two boats were launched and in a short time one of the harpooners was enabled to spear the fish. The second boat attacked the whale but was upset by a lash of its tail and the men thrown into the sea, one man being drowned, and another, James Bartley, having disappeared, could not be found. The whale was killed and *in a few hours* was lying by the ship's side and the crew were busy with axes and spades removing the blubber. *They worked all day and part of the night.* Next morning they attached some tackle to the stomach which was hoisted on the deck. The sailors were startled by something in it which gave spasmodic signs of life, and inside was found the missing sailor, doubled up and unconscious. He was laid on the deck and treated to a bath of sea water which soon revived him.[2]

Examples should not replace facts, but merely supplement them. Nothing is more frustrating to listen to than a dreary and silly recital of specific examples that prove nothing. For instance, a favorite ploy of some people in arguing against the welfare system is to cite case after case of some chiselers they heard about who eat steak and drive Cadillacs—all on the weekly dole. No doubt such cases do exist here and there, but citing examples of them does not prove that a majority of welfare recipients cheat, which is usually the underlying contention of this argument. "Hasty generalization" is the term logicians use to characterize this error in reasoning of drawing sweeping conclusions from one or two examples.

Examples alone merely establish the probability of an assertion, but they do not prove it. Because one sailor was swallowed by a sperm whale in 1771, and another in 1891, does not prove that Jonah was similarly engulfed. The examples merely indicate that something similar *could* have happened to Jonah. Assertions supported by examples alone should be cautiously worded to imply not proof but probability.

Sources for examples   These are more varied than the sources of cut-and-dried facts. You might find, for instance, supportive examples from the experiences of your own friends. If you were giving a speech about the inefficiency of federal bureaucracy, you might cite the case of an elderly acquaintance who has been badly mishandled by some office of the federal government. Perhaps you might even find an example from your own experiences. Beware, however, of building an argument on examples alone, or of making sweeping generalizations based on the recital of one or two instances.

Testimonials

The testimonial is a statement that cites the views, opinions, or experiences of someone else. Sometimes referred to as "witness evidence," or "authority opinion," testimonials, like examples, should be used to support rather than to replace hard facts. In citing testimonials, speakers are, in essence, trying to marshal favorable opinions behind their causes. The quality of the testimonial will consequently vary with the reputation and credentials of the person being quoted. Testimonials should be brief and to the point. Long, rambling testimonials will bore an audience.

Ordinarily, if the testimonial is from an authority, the authority should first be named and his or her credentials summarized before the opinion is quoted or paraphrased. Here is an example, taken from a speech decrying the quality of inner-city schools:

> John Goodlad, dean of the UCLA College of Education, concluded that the schools are "anything but the palaces of an affluent society." On the contrary, he writes, "They look more like the artifacts of a society that did not really care about its schools, a society that expressed its disregard by creating schools less suited to human habitation than its prisons."

The reason for such an introduction is obvious: to lend the authority's prestige to the testimonial.

If the persons being quoted are well known, then it is unnecessary to mention their credentials. Here is an example:

> When Harry Truman was asked about a President's power, he said that "the biggest power the President has . . . is the power to persuade people to do what they ought to do without having to be persuaded. And if a man thinks he's too big to do the necessary persuading, then he's in for trouble, and so is the country."

On the other hand, where unknown persons are being quoted because of some rare experience they have had, the introduction should specify enough about them to make their testimonials credible. Here is an example:

> Delsey Cortez of Albuquerque, New Mexico, was a state trooper for five years. Her record indicated that she was a stable and honest person. She sighted a UFO on one of her patrols. She described the spaceship as "taking off straight up" with a deafening roar.

Always bear in mind that the purpose of the introduction is simply to make the testimonial persuasive and intelligible. Long-winded introductions are usually unnecessary.

A testimonial may also be cited in paraphrase, rather than in an actual quotation. Here is an example:

> In every major city of the world the air is full of smoke and smog. When the Apollo 10 astronauts flew over Los Angeles, they still saw a yellow smudge even though they were about twenty-five thousand miles up.

Sources for testimonials   Testimonials can be gathered from a variety of sources. The opinions of various experts can be easily extracted from books and articles. Local authorities to whom you have access—such as doctors, teachers, and other professionals—can be interviewed for testimonials on their subject of expertise. The opinions of friends and acquaintances who have either a rare experience to share or an unusual expertise in some field can also be cited. You should not use the testimony of any person whose truthfulness is suspect or whose credentials are bogus.

Statistics and numbers

The word *statistics* comes from German, where it originally meant the materials that made up the political strength of a state. First used in English in the title *A Statistical Account of Scotland*—a volume published by Sir John Sinclair in 1791—*statistics* now refers to facts and data classified and expressed in numbers.

Though statistics and numbers are especially useful in depicting the nature of large groups or collections, inexperienced speakers should use them cautiously. Nothing chills an audience more quickly than a boring recital of statistics, especially statistics that describe a complicated relationship between two groups. Moreover, audiences of all kinds are traditionally suspicious of speakers who are too glib with figures.

Used sparingly, however, statistics and numbers can add a convincing precision to any speech. If, for instance, a speaker referred to general amounts rather than to specific quantities, the audience might find the assertions rather vague:

Some examples of resource use and environmental impact are seen in the following statements:

1. We are presently destroying massive acreages of land each year.

2. We throw away, use, and discharge every year into our environment:
   a. Mountains of cans
   b. Untold numbers of bottles
   c. Enough smoke to blanket the Plains States
   d. Enough carbon monoxide to kill millions
   e. A vast amount of hydrocarbon gas
   f. An incredible number of junked automobiles
   g. Huge amounts of nitrogen oxide
   h. Tons and tons of lead.

We use more oil, natural gas, coal, and other kinds of energy than any other country in the world.

The same statements made numerically are much more convincing:

> Some examples of resource use and environmental impact are seen in the following statements:
>
> 1. We are currently destroying agricultural land at the rate of 1,000,000 acres per year.
>
> 2. We discard, use, or discharge into the environment each year:
>
> a. 48,000,000,000 cans
> b. 26,000,000,000 bottles
> c. 142,000,000 tons of smoke
> d. 61,000,000 tons of carbon monoxide
> e. 16,000,000 tons of hydrocarbon gases
> f. 7,000,000 junked automobiles
> g. 6,000,000 tons of nitrogen oxide
> h. 210,000 tons of lead
>
> We use each day 4 gallons of oil, 300 cubic feet of natural gas, 15 pounds of coal, and smaller amounts of energy from other sources per person—eight times the world average.[3]

All statistics cited should be either preceded or followed by an explanation of their significance. Here is an example:

> The increasing size of the metropolitan area is compounding the problems local authorities must face. Since 1940, our population has grown by 50,000,000, the use of energy has quadrupled, disposable income has increased by 60 percent, yet our air supply remains the same. In such a setting air pollution is murder.

Sources for statistics and numbers   You should mention where your statistics came from, unless they were derived from an obviously verifiable source. The statistics cited above, for instance, are taken from census figures, which can easily be checked. But if you got your figures from some obscure or unpublished source, you should name it. Doing so gives any skeptics in your audience a chance to verify your figures.

Anecdotes

An anecdote is a brief story or episode, often humorous, that is told to add dramatic impact to an idea or proposition. Frequently, speakers use anecdotes as a lead-in to more serious topics. Here is an example of an anecdote used by a speaker just before he began a recital of some statistics:

> I never listen to a speaker launch out on one of those long discussions, filled with statistics of all kinds, or commit the same error myself, but that I think of the professor in a western university who taught mathematics and statistics. One day he was swimming, dressed in his bathing suit, at the edge of a swimming pool on the university campus when a beautiful coed accidentally dropped her camera into the deep end of the pool. She called to the elderly professor for help. He said he would be glad to dive down after the camera, but first wanted to know why she happened to choose him when there were so many young men within easy reach to do the job. She answered, "Professor, you have apparently forgotten me, but I am in your large statistics class. I have found that you can *go down deeper, stay down longer, and come up drier* than anyone I know."—I do not propose to go down too deep, stay down too long, or come up too dry with these statistics.

Anecdotes, of course, do not prove a speaker's point, but merely enliven it. Here, for instance, in his second address on energy, delivered over nationwide television on November 8, 1977, President Carter relates an anecdote:

> A few weeks ago in Detroit an unemployed steelworker told me something that may reflect the feelings of many of you. "Mr. President," he said, "I don't feel much like talking about energy and foreign policy. I am concerned about how I'm going to live. I can't be too concerned about other things when I have a 10-year-old daughter to raise and I don't have a job, and I'm 56 years old."
>
> Well, I understand how he felt, but I must tell you the truth, and the truth is that you cannot talk about our economic problems now or in the future without talking about energy.

This anecdote added a poignant, human touch to the speech.

Overuse of anecdotal material can give a speech a frivolous, folksy tone unsuitable to serious topics. Inexperienced speakers should therefore be especially careful in their use of anecdotes.

Diagrams and other graphics

In short speeches, such as are usually given in speech classes, diagrams often belabor the point, adding clutter rather than clarity to a presentation. Where the speech is long and the subject complicated, diagrams are useful, but such speeches are rarely given to fulfill the assignments of a speech class. It is possible, however, for a student to use a diagram in a short speech, especially a diagram that visually dramatizes a significant point.

Some commonsense rules should govern your use of diagrams and other graphics. First, diagrams and graphics used to illustrate a point should be instantly clear. It doesn't make sense to bring out an elaborate diagram or chart that will take you ten minutes to explain. Second, diagrams should illustrate the main point of your speech, not some secondary issue. For instance, it would have been pointless for the student giving the speech on the Shroud of Turin to present a diagram depicting the number of articles and books that have been written about the Shroud. The central idea of her speech was to tell what science has discovered about the Shroud, not to say how much material has been written about it. Third, diagrams should not introduce or explicate any point not covered in the speech itself. This point is self-evident; what speakers do not discuss in the speech they certainly do not need to show in a diagram.

Review of applications

Among the various kinds of details that can be used in support of an idea or claim are facts, definitions, examples, testimonials, statistics, anecdotes, and diagrams. Facts are accurate and verifiable assertions about reality; definitions specify what a thing is or what a term means; examples provide a listener with specific applications of an idea; testimonials cite the views or opinions of an expert or eyewitness; statistics provide a numerical overview of a subject; anecdotes add dramatic impact; and diagrams and graphics visually underscore a speaker's words. If used appropriately, each of these details can add immeasurably to a speaker's convincingness.

III. CAUTIONS

Our first and most urgent caution warns against the use of statistics that are so excessive as to bore an audience. The passage below—from a speech given by an Assistant Secretary of Education—uses statistics in a way that must have come close to boggling the audience.

> I received just before I left for Kansas a report from the National Center for Education Statistics which will be sent to the President showing that the salaries of women relative to men have not significantly improved either in private or public institutions of higher education. Women's salaries were 82.9 percent of men's salaries in 1972, and they were 83.2 percent in 1974. Women were also disadvantaged in the tenure situation where 26.7 percent of the women and 57 percent of the men had tenure. In academic rank, for example, in 1972 the total number of full women Professors was 9.8 percent and in 1974, 10.3 percent; women Associate Professors in 1972 numbered 16.3 percent and in 1974, 27.1 percent. The complete survey will be published at a later date, and I'd be very happy to send it to you.[4]

The point being made comes perilously close to being drowned in a sea of numbers.

Our second caution is a positive one: be specific. Beginning speakers often do not appreciate the value of calling things by their exact names. The speaker on the Shroud topic uses exact names and so invests her words with the specificness of authority. For example, she identifies the fabric pattern of the Shroud as "herringbone twill"; refers to the absence of "capillary action," which rules out a liquid medium; and says that the stains on the cloth responded the way blood does to "X-ray and ultraviolet tests." Each of these points could have been stated more vaguely or omitted altogether, to the detriment of the speech. The speaker could have said, for instance, "The material of the cloth is linen woven in a pattern known to the ancients." But with "herringbone twill" gone, this assertion does not pack the punch of the original.

Finally, be wary of misusing or overusing definitions. Not every term in a speech needs defining. Indeed, a definition is necessary only when the term is controversial or when the speaker is using it in a special way. For example, on page 21 of Chapter 2, the speaker needs to define *manners* because he is using the word in a special way. But if you were giving a speech, say, contrasting dogs and cats as household pets, it would obviously be silly to begin by defining what you mean by a dog or a cat. On the other hand, if your speech were on political satire in cartoons, you should probably briefly define what the word *satire* is generally held to mean. In sum, use your common sense to decide when you really need a definition and when you don't.

Review of cautions

Our first caution is a warning against misusing or overusing statistics. Speeches overloaded with numbers can easily bore an audience. Second, be as specific as you can in calling things by their exact names. Doing so can add the ring of authority to your speech. Finally, you should beware of overusing definitions, which are necessary only when you are using a word in a special way or when a term crucial to your speech is a controversial or easily misunderstood one.

Model speech

THE SHROUD OF TURIN

Testimony

One scientist insists it's a fake, but admits that he cannot prove it. Another thinks it's God's way of regenerating faith in a skeptical age. Both are referring to the Shroud of Turin, a piece of linen cloth 14 feet long and 3 feet wide that was first exhibited in the French town of Lirey in 1357 by a prominent knight who refused to say how he had come by it.

Definition

Imprinted on the Shroud by some unknown process is the image of a man with what appear to be blood spots ringing his forehead, puncture wounds through his wrists and feet, a puncture wound in his right side, and lacerations from a brutal whipping. The purpose of my speech is to tell you what science has found

Central idea

out about this religious relic, which believers say is the burial cloth of Jesus.

Numbers

In 1978, twenty-four scientists were given permission by the Catholic Church to study the Shroud. They examined it for 120 hours, using seventy-two crates of electronic gear. They took eighty photomosaics of it; processed sixty pairs of X-ray film; and

Facts

recorded thirty-six X-ray-fluorescence spectra, eighty-five infrared scans, and eighteen thermograms. Thirty-two samples were lifted off the linen with sticky tape.

What did the scientists find? First, that the image is on the individual fibrils themselves, and does not penetrate below the surface of the cloth. There is no capillary action of any kind, as would be expected if a liquid medium had been used. Second, that the image, when processed by a computer, is a three-dimensional one. Not even modern color photographs reveal three-dimensionality when computer-processed. Third, that there appears to be blood on the linen. The stains on the cloth responded to X-ray and ultraviolet tests the way blood does.

But the biggest mystery of all is how the image was formed. In 1898, quite by accident, a photographer discovered that the image was a negative one. When photographed, it reveals a positive image, showing far more realistic highlights and shadows than can be seen on the linen itself. This negative image was somehow put on the Shroud hundreds of years before the invention of photography.

Testimony

To date, science has been unable to explain how such an image was formed. All attempts to duplicate it have failed. Eric Jumper, an Air Force engineer, has written that the image could have been caused by radiation from "a very short molecular burst" of around "three seconds." Similar shadow images of plumbing valves and other objects were found on walls after the atomic bombing of Hiroshima. What no one can say, however, is how an atomic shadow could have been imprinted on a piece of cloth first discovered in 1357.

Facts

If the Shroud of Turin is a forgery, it is a fiendishly skillful one. The material of the cloth is linen, handwoven in a herringbone twill—a pattern known to the ancients. It was found to contain pollen grains from plants common in areas around the Dead Sea and Palestine. Whoever might have forged the Shroud also knew something about Roman crucifixions we did not. For the Shroud's victim was crucified not through the palms, as in the biblical account, but through the wrists. It was only in 1931 that a French surgeon demonstrated that nails driven through the palms will not support a cadaver on a cross. And in 1968, near Jerusalem, archeologists unearthed the bones of a man named Jehohanan, an actual crucifixion victim. He had spike wounds through the wrists—exactly like the wounds on the Shroud.

Example { Scientists continue to study the Shroud. And the Shroud continues to mystify all who have examined it. When Ray Rogers, a thermal chemist and archeologist with the Los Alamos Scientific Laboratory, first heard about the Shroud in 1976, he said, "Give me twenty minutes and I'll have this thing shot full of holes." He's still studying it.

BIBLIOGRAPHY

Murphy, Cullen. "Shreds of Evidence." *Harper's,* November 1981, pp. 42–65.

"The Mystery of the Shroud of Turin Challenges 20th-Century Science." *Science,* 21 July 1978, pp. 235–239.

Thomsen, Dietrick E. "The Shroud of Turin: A Shroud of Unknowing." *Science News* 1978, pp. 442–455.

"Turin Shroud Placed 800 Years Closer to Christ by Duke Prof." *Atlanta Constitution,* 28 January 1982, Sec. C, p.1, col. 3.

Walsh, John. *The Shroud.* London: W. H. Allen, 1963.

Weaver, Kenneth F. "The Mystery of the Shroud." *National Geographic,* June 1980, pp. 730–72.

Wilson, Ian. *The Shroud of Turin.* New York: Doubleday, 1978.

EXERCISES

1. Arrange the statements within each group of assertions in order of specificity, from the most general to the most specific:

    a. The *Titanic* was the biggest ship of her day.
    b. The *Titanic* was 882.5 feet long and 92.5 feet in extreme breadth.
    c. The *Titanic* was a big ship.

    d. Boswell wrote a biography, *The Life of Johnson,* which is considered a classic of the genre.
    e. Boswell wrote a book.
    f. Boswell wrote a biography.

    g. Love and marriage are traceable back through millions of years of human evolution.
    h. Love and marriage have been around for a long time.
    i. Love and marriage are the products of 35 million years of human evolution.

j. In October 1957, a sunspot count revealed 263. One sunspot was observed for 200 days, from June to December.

k. In the fall a few years ago, scientists noticed a lot of sunspots. One lasted a long time.

l. Twenty years ago, scientists counted over 200 sunspots. One sunspot was observed for over a half a year.

m. People have lived at as high an altitude as 21,200 feet.

n. The Tibetan herders live in the settlement of Barudusk-sum, 21,200 feet above sea level.

o. Some people have been known to live at very high altitudes.

p. During its best year, the total worldwide sales of General Motors reached a staggering sum.

q. In 1975, General Motors' sales worldwide were over $34 billion.

r. During its peak year of 1975, General Motors' worldwide sales totalled $35,724,911,215.

s. The silly feats people will do for publicity are astonishing. One man, for instance, got his name into the *Guinness Book of Records* by devouring an enormous number of franks in a remarkably short time.

t. The silly feats people will do for publicity are astonishing. One man, for instance, got his name into the *Guinness Book of Records* by devouring 20 franks in less than 4 minutes.

u. The silly feats people will do for publicity are astonishing. One man, for instance, got his name into the *Guinness Book of Records* by devouring 20 2-oz. franks in 3 minutes, 33 seconds on March 3, 1976.

2. Identify the kinds of supporting detail used in the following assertions.

a. Chemistry is that branch of science which has the task of investigating the materials out of which the universe is made. . . . Chemistry is concerned not only with the composition of . . . substances but also with their inner structure.

b. At the turn of the century, infectious diseases were the primary health menace to this nation. Acute respiratory conditions such as pneumonia and influenza were the major killers. Tuberculosis, too, drained the nation's vitality. Gastrointestinal infections decimated the child population.

   c. People can reduce and lose weight. Alfred Hitchcock went from 365 lbs. to a weight of 200 lbs. Jackie Gleason scaled down from 280 lbs. to 221 lbs.

   d. While the professional man is engaged in the struggle for professional success, his wife may find herself in what Betty Friedan called "the sexual ghetto," with no one to talk to over 3-feet tall.

   e. The culture gap can also be applied to the school curriculum. In an inner-city parochial school, an old Catholic nun—in all the pomp and circumstance of theological education—spent the entire semester grinding her definition of God into the minds of her third-grade class. "God is a Supreme Being," she said over and over. "God is a Supreme Being." One day she decided to test the results of her efforts. "Tommy," she said, "tell us who God is." And Tommy stood up and very proudly announced, "God is a Green Bean."

   f. Divorce rates have been rising in all Western countries. In many countries the rates are rising even faster than in the United States. In 1910 the divorce rate for the United States was 87 per 1000 marriages. In 1965 the rate had risen to an estimated figure of well over 300 per 1000 in many parts of the country.

NOTES

[1] Clarence Darrow, "Why I Am an Agnostic," symposium on religion, Columbus, Ohio, 1929.

[2] Victor B. Scheffer, *The Year of the Whale* (New York: Scribner's, 1969).

[3] Arthur H. Doerr, "The Bounds of Earth," speech given before Pensacola Home Builders Association, Pensacola, Florida, 6 December 1973.

[4] Virginia Y. Trotter, speech given to the Academic Women Conference, Kansas State University, 15 February 1975.

Making an outline

I. PRINCIPLES

People have fallible memories. Most of us at one time or another have sat squirming in our seats, dying to be called on by a teacher or a moderator. Once called on, however, we mumble and falter, our splendid point forgotten, its wonderful phrasing lost. As soon as the discussion moves on, we remember what we had intended to say, and fly into a rage at our forgetfulness. Even the best speakers have had a similar experience. Memory lapses occur under the pressure of the moment; points and passages studiously researched and revised are abruptly forgotten once the speaker faces the audience. The speaker mumbles, coughs, and finally ends up improvising.

Anguish of this sort is easily preventable if you use an *outline*. You can carry the outline with you to the podium, and glance at it every so often to jog your memory. The outline simply plots out what you intend to say and how you intend to say it. In sum, the outline provides a thumbnail sketch of your entire speech.

Properly worded, the central idea can predict the principal parts of a speech, making outlining much easier. Here is an example:

Central idea: The hot dog is so saturated with chemicals, so contaminated with bacteria, so puffy with gristle, fat, and water, and so lacking in protein that it is nutritionally worthless.

The central idea tells the speaker the sequence of points to be covered. Contained in the central idea is the gist of an outline. Here are the principal topics, in sequence, that will be covered in the speech:

    I. The chemical content of hot dogs
    II. The bacterial content of hot dogs
    III. The gristle, fat, and water content of hot dogs
    IV. The protein content of hot dogs

Notice how easily the topics of the speech can be extracted from the wording of the central idea. You should likewise word your central ideas in such a way as to enunciate an obvious and "outlineable" pattern to your speeches.

To predict the topics of a speech, a central idea need not be longwinded or cumbersome. Consider this central idea.

Central idea: Good writing is clear, vivid, and appropriate.

This rather straightforward central idea nevertheless contains within it the obvious gist of an outline. Clearly the speaker would be obligated to speak on the following sequence of topics:

    I. The clarity of good writing
    II. The vividness of good writing
    III. The appropriateness of good writing

The speaker simply has to accumulate definitions and examples that illustrate the clarity, vividness, and appropriateness of good writing.

The well-drafted central idea always contains, if not obvious topic divisions, at least one or two *key words* that are divisible into the major headings of an outline. Consider, for instance, these two examples:

There are numerous <u>advantages</u> to riding a bicycle.

The feminist movement will <u>improve</u> the <u>lives</u> of <u>men</u>.

The key words are underlined. In the first example, the key word is *advantages*. The speaker is obligated, in the speech, to enumerate the advantages of bicycle riding. Here is an outline, based on a subdivision of the key word *advantages:*

I. Advantages of economy

    A. Bicycles are inexpensive to buy.
    B. Bicycles cost little to operate.
    C. Bicycles depreciate very little.

II. Advantages of maneuverability

    A. Bicycles are maneuverable in traffic.
    B. Bicycles are easy to park.
    C. Bicycles can be ridden almost everywhere.

III. Advantages of exercise

    A. Bicycle riding tones the muscles.
    B. Bicycle riding strengthens the heart.
    C. Bicycle riding promotes weight loss.

In the second example, the key words are *improve*, *lives*, and *men*. Following is an outline based on a subdivision of these words:

I. Improvements in social life

    A. Men will be freed from a number of social expectations.
    B. Men will have more role choices.

II. Improvements in business life

    A. Men will be free to choose from a wider range of careers.
    B. Men will be freed from the compulsion to succeed.

III. Improvements in physical life

    A. Men are likely to live longer.
    B. Men will probably lead fuller lives.

While other headings are possible, the principle of creating an outline remains the same: subdivision of the central idea into a series of smaller topics.

Outline format

Outlines have a visual format that can be taken in at a glance. Speakers ordinarily do not plop an outline of their speech down on a podium and then read from it. Instead, they glance casually at the outline every now and again to assure themselves that they are dealing with the major ideas of their speech in proper sequence. The permissible classroom uses of an outline will vary from teacher to teacher. Some teachers require students to construct a formal outline and submit it, along with the written text of the speech, after the speech has been delivered. Other teachers regard the outline merely as a convenience to the student and neither read nor evaluate it. Whatever the practice in your class, you should become familiar with the conventional outline format.

Main ideas are designated by Roman numerals and aligned on the page. Subideas, branching off these main ideas, are designated by capital letters and are also aligned with each other. Examples of these subideas are marked by Arabic numerals, while details supporting the examples are indicated by lowercase letters. The outline format looks like this:

> I. Main Idea
>   A. Subidea
>   1. Example
>   a. Detail
>   B. Subidea
>   1. Example
>   a. Detail
>
> II. Main Idea
>   A. Subidea
>   1. Example
>   a. Detail
>   B. Subidea
>   1. Example
>   a. Detail

In sum, major ideas are slotted to the left, and less important ideas are slotted to the right. This visual format enables a speaker to take in, at a glance, the structure of the entire speech.

Review of principles

Speakers use outlines to plot out in advance the points they intend to cover in a speech. Properly worded, the central idea can predict the principal topics of a speech and make outlining easier. Outlines can be created by dividing the key words of a central idea into a series of smaller topics. While the permissible classroom use of an outline will vary from teacher to teacher, all outlines more or less observe the same visual format of slotting major ideas to the left, and less important ones to the right.

II. APPLICATIONS

There are several ways of outlining a speech, depending on the topic. Some topics naturally lend themselves to one kind of outline; other topics may be outlined equally well in a different arrangement. To prepare an outline, you must first have a central idea and the supporting materials you intend to use. Listed below are various arrangements in which a speech topic may be outlined.

Topical arrangement of headings

By far the commonest outline is the arrangement in logical order of topics. The speaker simply divides the central idea into smaller, manageable topic headings. The two outlines given earlier, on the advantages of bicycle riding and on the improvements men can expect from the feminist movement, are both topically arranged. Here is another example:

Central idea: Extremes in temperature can have dangerous effects on mountain climbers.

    I. The dangerous effects of extreme heat
      A. Heat exhaustion
      B. Heat stroke
      C. Heat cramps

   II. The dangerous effects of extreme cold
      A. Surface frostbite
      B. Body numbness
      C. Drowsiness

In making a topical outline, you must decide on the most reasonable and logical way of subdividing your central idea. Once you have chosen a principle for the subdivision, you should consistently observe it throughout the entire outline. Consider, for instance, the following outline:

Central idea: Cigarette smoking adversely affects virtually every system of the body.

    I. Adverse effects on the cardiovascular system
      A. The heart beats faster.
      B. The blood vessels constrict.

    II. Adverse effects on the digestive system
      A. The stomach secretes excess gastric acids.
      B. The appestat malfunctions.

    III. Low tar and nicotine cigarettes are better for the smoker.
      A. There is less tar and nicotine to irritate the bronchi and lungs.
      B. The level of nicotine in the blood is gradually lowered.

    IV. Adverse effects on the respiratory system
      A. The bronchial cilia are paralyzed.
      B. The bronchial sacs lose their elasticity.

Heading III is glaringly out of place. The student chose, as the most logical division of the central idea, to systematically outline the adverse effects of cigarettes on each system of the body. Heading III simply does not fit in with this scheme of outlining. It is neither predicted by the central ideal nor anticipated by the audience. The inclusion of this topic therefore violates the principle on which the outline is based. This is the way the outline should look:

    I. Adverse effects on the cardiovascular system
      A. The heart beats faster.
      B. The blood vessels constrict.

    II. Adverse effects on the digestive system
      A. The stomach secretes excess gastric acids.
      B. The appestat malfunctions.

    III. Adverse effects on the respiratory system
      A. The bronchial cilia are paralyzed.
      B. The bronchial sacs lose their elasticity.

The topical arrangement of the headings in an outline is especially suitable when the central idea consists of obvious and separate parts. Consider this central idea:

The health resources of America are inefficiently distributed and poorly organized.

The logical division that immediately suggests itself is a split of the speech into its two principal parts:

    I. Inefficient distribution of health resources
   II. Poor organization of health resources

Common sense and your own innate sense of logic should dictate the most suitable principle for creating a topical outline.

Chronological arrangement of headings

Some central ideas lend themselves well to an arrangement of headings based upon progressive chronology, such as:

> Throughout the years, the definition of the *second* has been constantly refined.

Implicit in this central idea is the notion of progressing chronology— exactly the principle most suitable for outlining speeches about historical subjects. Here is an outline based on a chronological arrangement of topics:

    I. In 1884, the second was defined according to the daily rotation of the earth.

   II. In 1960, the second was defined according to the solar orbit of the earth.

  III. In 1967, the second was defined according to the wobble of an electron.

The principal headings in this outline are derived from a time arrangement—an arrangement especially suitable for speeches about historical subjects.

Spatial arrangement of headings

Central ideas that describe a city, a country, or other place are especially suited to an arrangement of headings based on space.

Central idea: Jamaica, called the "pearl of the Caribbean," is a variegated island.

I. The eastern end of the island, comprising the county of Surrey, is characterized by rolling grass plains and a naturally sheltered deep-water harbor.

II. The central portion of the island, comprising the county of Middlesex, is mountainous and heavily wooded.

III. The western end of the island, comprising the county of Cornwall, presents a most spectacular meeting of land and ocean, boasting some of the loveliest stretches of beaches in the world.

The speech, in its description of the island, is obviously arranged to move from east to west. An audience would immediately grasp this arrangement and be easily able to follow it.

Problem/solution arrangement of headings

Another approach is to outline the headings of a central idea in a problem/solution sequence. First the speaker enumerates and catalogs the problem; then the speaker proposes a solution and elaborates on it. Here is an example:

Central idea: The quality of the school cafeteria service could be vastly improved if it were managed by the Student Council.

Problems:

I. The school cafeteria serves poor quality food.
   A. Complaints about the cafeteria food are received every day at the Student Council office.
   B. Last year, four students were poisoned by tuna sandwiches served in the cafeteria.

II. The cafeteria operates at hours inconvenient to the student body.
   A. The cafeteria opens too late to serve students who have early classes.
   B. The cafeteria closes too early to serve students who have night classes.

III. The problem of poor quality food and inconvenient operating hours could be solved with Student Council management of the cafeteria.

Solutions:

A. The Student Council would be able to monitor and control cafeteria food quality.
B. The Student Council would be able to establish operating hours convenient to the students.
C. The student body would have indirect control, through their elected representatives, over the running of the cafeteria.

This rather obvious arrangement is easy for an audience to follow. Moreover, it allows the speaker to exert considerable control over the structure and direction of the speech.

Cause/effect arrangement of headings

Finally, the headings of an outline may be arranged in a cause/effect sequence. Consider this central idea and outline:

Central idea: The diet of Americans is regarded as a contributing cause of cancer.

Cause:

I. Americans consume too much red meat.
   A. Americans consume 35 percent of the world's annual meat supply.
   B. High meat consumption correlates with a high incidence of colon and breast cancers.

II. Americans consume too little raw food fiber and roughage.
   A. Some 40 percent of the American diet consists of processed foods that, according to the Senate Select Committee on Nutrition and Human Needs, are lacking in natural fiber.
   B. Lower intake of food fiber correlates with a higher incidence of intestinal cancer.

Effect:

III. Partly because of our diet, we suffer nearly the highest incidence of cancer in the world.
   A. Cancer is the number 2 killer of Americans.
   B. Cancer costs Americans nearly $2 billion per year.

The speech is divided roughly into two parts: a cataloging of cause, followed by a recital of effects. But the order could just have effectively been reversed: a recital of effects, followed by a discussion of cause, as in the following example:

Effect: $\left\{\begin{array}{l}\end{array}\right.$ I. Partly because of our diet, we suffer nearly the highest incidence of cancer in the world.
  A. Cancer is the number 2 killer of Americans.
  B. Cancer costs Americans nearly $2 billion per year.

II. Americans consume too much red meat.
  A. Americans consume 35 percent of the world's annual meat supply.
  B. High meat consumption correlates with a high incidence of colon and breast cancers.

Cause: III. Americans consume too little raw food fiber and roughage.
  A. Some 40 percent of the American diet consists of processed foods that, according to the Senate Select Committee on Nutrition and Human Needs, are lacking in natural fiber.
  B. Lower intake of food fiber correlates with a higher incidence of intestinal cancer.

Naturally, this particular outline sequence is especially suited to speeches that set out to either enumerate causes or to catalog effects.

Outline headings and oral paragraphs

Students are frequently puzzled about the relationship between the individual headings in an outline and particular paragraphs in a speech. No exact formula exists, nor is one necessary. Major subdivisions in an outline are generally treated as separate paragraphs, but even this rule is not consistently observed.

Basically, you should try to give an idea the approximate emphasis it has in the outline. In other words, a minor detail should not consume entire paragraphs; a major idea should not be carelessly dismissed in one short sentence. In the excitement of speaking, you could easily become fixated on some minor point and ramble on endlessly about it, resulting in a lopsided speech and a bewildered audience. Following an outline, which more or less indicates the proportional importance of each point in the speech, will prevent you from making that mistake.

To illustrate the relationship between outline entries and paragraphs, we present the following example of an outline along with two complete paragraphs derived from it.

Central idea: Throughout the years, the definition of the *second* has been constantly refined.

    I. An early definition of the second was agreed on in 1884.
        A. The second was defined as the time it took the earth to complete 1/86,400 of its daily rotation.
        B. The earth wobbled as it rotated, losing as much as 1/10 of a second annually and negating the 1884 definition.

    II. The second was redefined in 1960.
        A. The second was defined as the time it took the earth to complete 1/31,556,925.9747 of its solar orbit.
        B. Atmospheric properties of the earth made the measurement of solar orbit inexact, negating the 1960 definition.

    III. The second was redefined again in 1967.
        A. The second was defined as equal to 9,192,631,770 wobbles of a cesium electron.
        B. Time loss of only one 10 billionth of a second per day made the 1967 definition amazingly accurate.

Here are the oral paragraphs:

An early definition of the second was internationally agreed on in 1884. This definition was rather simply arrived at. It was believed that the earth made one complete rotation on its own axis every twenty-four hours. Twenty-four hours are equal to 86,400 seconds. The second was therefore defined as the time it takes the earth to complete 1/86,400 of its daily rotation.

This definition, however, was soon found to be inadequate with the discovery that the earth wobbles as it rotates. In fact, the earth resembles an unsteady, spinning top. It does not religiously complete one rotation every 86,400 seconds, as was assumed. Sometimes it is early, and sometimes late. Its rotation is affected by earthquakes, volcanic eruptions, and other large-scale natural catastrophes. On an average, it loses about 1/10 of a second per year. The definition of the second according to the rotation of the earth was therefore abandoned as inaccurate.

In sum, the entries of the outline should be transformed into reasonable oral-paragraph equivalents. For more on the construction of oral paragraphs, see Chapter 9.

Review of applications

Depending on the topic, the headings of an outline may be arranged in logical order; in chronological order; in spatial order; in problem/solution order; or in cause/effect order. For the outline to be a useful guide to the speaker, each entry in the outline should reflect the approximate emphasis the subtopic will receive in the speech.

III. CAUTIONS

The outline is a means to an end, not an end in itself. The point is to make a good speech—one that will impart your message to your audience. If the speech you are giving from your outline is boring the audience, don't be afraid to throw away the outline—no matter how meticulously prepared it may be—and improvise. You may have chosen an approach that simply does not appeal to your particular audience. The point is to remain sensitive to audience feedback and to modify the speech if it becomes apparent that your approach is not working. Our first caution then is simply this: don't lock yourself in to any outline. If your outlined speech is not not getting through, change it.

In preparing the outline itself, be sure to indent its entries properly. A badly prepared outline that's difficult to read will only make it harder for you to keep your mind on the order of topics. Also, don't be afraid to highlight any particular entry you may want to emphasize. Use a light-colored magic marker if you like. Regard the outline as a memorandum intended for your eyes only. If you have to turn in a written outline to the teacher, prepare two copies: one that you can mark up as much as you need to, the other that is neat and unmarked, for the teacher to read.

Finally, we would caution you to make the entries of your outline parallel. Experience has shown that parallel entries are easier to read at a glance than entries that are randomly worded. Consider, for instance, the following outline entries:

Central idea: Good writing is clear, vivid, and appropriate.

      I. The clarity of good writing

     II. Good writing is vivid.

    III. The appropriateness of good writing

Obviously, such an outline will not be simple to read, especially by a speaker under stress. Contrast this with the outline below, whose entries have parallel wording:

      I. The clarity of good writing

     II. The vividness of good writing

    III. The appropriateness of good writing

The outline with parallel entries is far easier to read at a glance.

Review of cautions

Don't be afraid to deviate from your outline if audience feedback tells you that your prepared speech is not getting through. Do properly indent the entires of the outline to reflect the relative importance of each topic. And, finally, do make the entries of the outline parallel so that they'll be readable at a glance.

EXERCISES

1. What obvious and logical divisions could be made of the following central ideas?

    a. The primary strokes in tennis are the ground stroke, the volley, the lob, and the overhead smash.

    b. Flying a small plane is expensive, exciting, and risky.

    c. Modern poetry is either incomprehensible or ideological.

    d. Blackjack systems are difficult to master and nearly impossible to practice under casino play conditions.

    e. The shark is a necessary and useful predator.

2. Identify the "key words" that could be subdivided in the following central ideas to create an outline.

    a. Heart disease is a killer.

    b. Cancer can be prevented.

    c. Stocks are a risky investment.

    d. Acupuncture is an effective treatment.

3. What kind of arrangement would you use to outline the following central ideas?

    a. The discovery of penicillin took place in many small steps over the years.

    b. The high crime rate in the United States could be solved by the right social programs.

    c. The state of California is made up of at least three distinct climatic regions.

    d. Houseplants should be well aired, well exposed, and well watered.

    e. Air pollution is a major cause of respiratory illness in urban areas.

4. Criticize the following brief outlines:

    a. *Central idea:* The natal horoscope of John Dillinger predicted him to be a violent, rash, and vengeful man.

        I. The natal horoscope of John Dillinger predicted that he would be violent.

        II. If the Lady in Red hadn't betrayed Dillinger, he might never have been caught.

        III. John Dillinger was a rash man.

        IV. The natal horoscope of John Dillinger predicted that he would be vengeful.

    b. *Central idea:* The Heimlich method of saving a choking victim is effective, easy to master, and can save lives.

        I. The Heimlich method of saving a choking victim is effective.

        II. People usually choke because they eat too fast and bite off more than they can swallow.

III. The Heimlich method of saving a choking victim is easy to master.

IV. The Heimlich method can save the life of a choking victim.

Constructing oral paragraphs

I. PRINCIPLES

Paragraph, a term originally meaning "something written besides," comes from medieval manuscripts, where a marginal mark was used to indicate a new idea in the text. This mark eventually evolved into an indentation, and the paragraph became a square block of print on the page. When we see a new paragraph, we automatically expect either the introduction of a new idea or some other substantial shift in the discussion.

The paragraph, though a manuscript convention, is also used in speeches. Good speakers do not ramble interminably, but speak in distinctive, though invisible, blocks of thought very similar to the written paragraph. Verbal emphasis, enunciation, and pauses are used to signal these oral paragraphs.

Structure of the oral paragraph

The oral paragraph, like its written counterpart, is usually structured to proceed either from the general to the specific, or from the specific to the general. Here is an example of a paragraph with a structure proceeding from the general to the specific: a generalization is made, which is then supported by specific details.

113

Generalization { All the chemicals added to hot dogs still haven't made them pure. For example, in tests conducted on hot dogs by *Consumer Reports,* only two brands tested did not exceed the maximum allowable level of contamination—10,000 bacteria per gram of meat. Forty percent of the samples analyzed—and all national *Specific details* { brands were tested—had already begun to spoil, though they came straight off the shelves and were air-shipped under refrigeration to the lab. Rodent hairs and insect parts were also found in all the samples.

In this example, the generalization is made as a declarative sentence. But it can also be made as a question, which it often is in a speech. Here is an example of an oral paragraph whose generalization is worded as a question, which is then answered by the supporting details:

Generalization worded as a question { What does it really mean to be a hemophiliac? The first indication comes in early childhood when a small scratch may bleed for hours. By the time the hemophiliac reaches school age, he begins to suffer from internal bleeding into muscles, joints, the stomach, the kidneys. This latter type is far more serious, for external wounds can usually be stopped in minutes with topical thromboplastin or a pressure bandage. But internal bleeding can be checked only *Supporting details* { by changes in the blood by means of transfusions or plasma injections. If internal bleeding into a muscle or joint goes unchecked repeatedly, muscle contraction and bone deformity inevitably result. My crooked left arm, the built-up heel on my right shoe, and the full length brace on my left leg offer mute but undeniable testimony to that fact. Vocal evidence you hear; weak tongue muscles are likely to produce defective L and R sounds.[1]

Other paragraphs are structured to proceed from the specific to the general. Supporting details are first given, and a generalization then drawn. Here is an example:

Supporting details { She was 882.5 feet long, 92.5 feet wide, weighed 46,328 tons at launching, and boasted a hull divided into 16 watertight compartments. She had two triple expansion reciprocating steam engines, capable of driving her along at 21 knots with virtually no vibration. She had seven grand staircases, two huge leaded

Generalization { glass skylights, a gymnasium, hospital, swimming pool, library, post office, Turkish bath, and squash-rac-quets court. <u>The *Titanic* was her name, and she was built for comfort, safety, and size, not for speed.</u>

The generalization found in a paragraph is its topic idea and contains an assertion that the supporting details amplify, reinforce, prove, or otherwise document. The topic idea that cannot be ade-quately documented or supported in a single paragraph will some-times be developed in two or three paragraphs. Here is an example taken from a speech titled "The Unmentionable Diseases." The speaker has just described the ravages of venereal diseases, citing alarming statistics on their incidence.

Generalization worded as a question { <u>Why are these statistics so staggering if penicillin was such a wonderful discovery?</u> According to Dr. Neal E. Baxter, a Bloomington physician who was the head of the V.D. research in Monroe County for sev-eral years, the first factor in this spreading problem is the mobility of the population and the loosening and decline in morals today. One sophisticated syphilitic had contacts with 171 people in 7 states and 5 for-eign countries. The free-and-easy attitude toward morals is easily indicated by the Kinsey surveys, which originated at Indiana University. These reveal that a large number of American adolescents indulge in sex-ual experimentation—kissing, necking, petting—be-fore they are 15 years of age. Premarital intercourse increases in frequency as adolescence progresses. By the age of 20, about 75% of the males and 40% of the females have had sexual intercourse. Promiscuity does not stop at this age level, however, as a random survey of Kinsey's pointed out that over 25% of 6,000 women interviewed had had extramarital relations before age 40.

Supporting details that develop and answer the question

More supporting details { The second factor contributing to the rise of V.D. is the false public confidence in antibiotics. Since pen-icillin has been termed a "miracle" drug, many peo-ple, so confident in its "cure-all," have waited too long before treatment and have tried to merely get some penicillin pills from their druggist. Further research for possible cures was ended by the discovery of pen-icillin because Federal appropriations were cut off.

Further answers
given in
this paragraph
{
The final contributing factors to the rise of V.D. are widespread ignorance and public indifference. In 1966, Dr. Daniel Rosenblatt of New York City's Health Research Council found that one-half of the students in two city colleges did not know how V.D. was contracted. In a national health test conducted by CBS television, over two-thirds of the entire population had little knowledge of venereal diseases, their symptoms, cures, or possible consequences.[2]

The topic idea developed over two or three paragraphs is, of course, more commonly found in longer speeches. In shorter speeches, the topic idea is generally developed within a single paragraph.

Review of principles

The paragraph, a written convention that evolved from medieval manuscripts, is also used in speeches. Oral paragraphs are usually structured to proceed from the specific to the general; some, however, have the opposite structure—from the general to the specific. The generalization in a paragraph is its topic idea—the main point that its details establish or support. In shorter speeches, a topic idea is usually developed in a single paragraph; but in longer speeches, a topic idea may be developed over two or more paragraphs.

II. APPLICATIONS

You have done research on your subject, made the notes you need, and tentatively sketched an outline of the speech. The next step is to transform your notes into individual oral paragraphs. Exactly how much writing you will have to do depends on your teacher. Some teachers require students to actually compose the speech on paper and then deliver it before the class. Other teachers expect their students to speak extemporaneously from their notes and outline. A third group of teachers require their students to deliver the speech from their notes and outline, and then to submit the speech in written form. Your teacher will make it clear exactly what you are required to do.

If you have done the research properly, the process of turning

your notes into paragraphs can be rather automatic, for the quality
of a paragraph invariably depends on the quality of its details. Packed
with interesting details, the paragraph will seem fresh and lively;
lacking such details, the paragraph will sound wishy-washy and dull.
Nor can clever wording or cute images compensate for the emptiness
of a paragraph. In sum, if you wish to construct good oral paragraphs, you must first be in possession of the facts. Here are some
suggestions for constructing oral paragraphs.

Develop a single idea in each paragraph

Speakers have to be especially careful to restrict the coverage of
their paragraphs to a single, comprehensible idea, or they run the
risk of baffling their audiences. We suggest that you word the generalizations of your paragraphs to express a single idea that can be
adequately documented with supporting details. Here are two examples, one wrong, the other right:

> *Poor:*   There are five venereal diseases, all of which can cause
> death, but penicillin can cure them if it is used early
> enough.

The generalization commits the speaker to discuss two separate
ideas: kinds of venereal disease and penicillin as a cure. It is impossible to support both topics adequately in a single paragraph without
thoroughly confusing the audience. Poorly worded generalizations are
the commonest flaw of student paragraphs. But it is a flaw that can
be easily corrected.

> *Better:*   There are five venereal diseases, all of which can cause
> death. Three of these have been eliminated by modern
> medicine, while the other two, syphilis and gonorrhea,
> are on the rise once more all over the world. Both of
> these diseases are mainly contracted through sexual re-
> lations. These germs spread to all parts of the body, and,
> therefore, anything the infected person uses is possibly
> an immediate carrier. These germs can spread to an-
> other human by an open cut if it comes in close contact
> with the germs of the infected person.[3]

Word generalizations to interpret supporting details

The purpose of the generalization in a paragraph is not only to further the discussion but also to interpret the supporting details. Uninterpreted details are meaningless. It is not enough to simply pack a paragraph with facts; the audience must also be told what the facts mean. Here are two examples:

> *Poor:*   Last year I was disturbed to read an article in the *Saturday Evening Post* entitled, "Youth—The Cool Generation." It was written by Dr. Gallup and Evan Hill and was based on 3,000 interviews with young people up to the age of 22. The article stated that the typical youth will settle for low success rather than risk high failure; that he has little spirit of adventure; that he wants little because he has so much, and is unwilling to risk what he has.

One might ask, so what? The generalization of a paragraph should answer exactly such a question.

> *Better:*   The idea of security seems to have grown so rapidly in recent years that the spirit of risk-taking—historically the dominant mark of youth—has become somewhat dulled. Last year I was disturbed to read an article in the *Saturday Evening Post* entitled, "Youth—The Cool Generation." It was written by Dr. Gallup and Evan Hill and was based on 3,000 interviews with young people up to the age of 22. The article stated that the typical youth will settle for low success rather than risk high failure; that he has little spirit of adventure; that he wants little because he has so much, and is unwilling to risk what he has.[4]

The uninterpreted detail is not worth giving. Do not, therefore, simply stockpile details in your paragraphs. Use details to support your generalizations; use generalizations to interpret your details.

Avoid mixed constructions

Mixed constructions are sentences that begin with one grammatical pattern, then abruptly and pointlessly switch to another. The human ear is accustomed to certain regularities in the construction of sentences. For instance, when we hear this first half of a sentence:

When it snows . . . ———⟶

we anticipate this kind of completion:

⟵——— . . . children often throw snowballs in the streets.

We do not, however, expect to hear something like this:

When it snows . . . the throwing of snowballs in the streets by children often takes place.

Obviously, this sentence, by departing unnecessarily from the anticipated pattern of completion, is more difficult to understand.

Consider, as another example, this opening to a sentence:

Charlene's whistling between her teeth . . . ———⟶

Ordinarily, we anticipate the sentence to end thus:

⟵——— . . . often irritates her husband.

We do not, however, expect:

Charlene's whistling between her teeth her husband is often irritated at.

Some mixed constructions are more subtle. Consider, for instance, the following sentence:

When her builders launched the *Titanic,* she was the largest ship afloat.

In the first half of the sentence "builders" is the subject; in the second half *Titanic* is the subject. Notice how much easier to understand and more straightforward this sentence is when written this way:

When the *Titanic* was launched, she was the largest ship afloat.

The improved clarity is the result of both halves of the sentence having the same subject—the *Titanic* in the first half, and a pronoun that refers to the *Titanic* in the second half.

Your own language instincts will have to guide you in avoiding mixed constructions. If you aim at constructing straightforward oral sentences, you should have no great difficulty with mixed constructions. Often the speaker who tries to sound highfalutin and grand is the one whose constructions are perplexingly mixed.

Use pronouns that refer to unmistakable antecedents

Pronouns should never be used unless their antecedents are unmistakably clear. Here is an example of faulty pronoun reference:

Poor: To make the *Titanic* unsinkable, her builders equipped her with sixteen watertight compartments. They knew that she could stay afloat even if they were ruptured.

Pronouns have a tendency to attach themselves to the closest noun. Though the first *they* is meant to refer to the "builders," it could be misconstrued to stand for "watertight compartments." The second *they* is nearly incomprehensible, and listeners would have a great deal of trouble understanding what it refers to.

Better: To make the *Titanic* unsinkable, her builders equipped her with sixteen watertight compartments. The builders knew that the *Titanic* could stay afloat, even if her watertight compartments were ruptured.

Beware of confusion between the expletive *it* and the pronoun *it*. Here is a sentence that uses *it* as an expletive:

It is the men who must pay.

Here is a sentence that confuses the expletive *it* with the pronoun:

Poor: The object is cylindrical and blue. It can be said that it weighs more than it ought to.

The first *it* is an expletive; the second and third are pronouns.

Better: The object is cylindrical, blue, and weighs more than it ought to.

Use transitional expressions to help a listener follow your ideas

Transitional expressions are often used between oral paragraphs to move the discussion smoothly from one idea to another. But they are also used within a paragraph to make it easier for listeners to follow the flow of ideas.

> <u>Although</u> we students do bring many of our problems to campus with us, college can easily increase the intensity of some problems and create new ones. <u>So, basically,</u> on the college campus there are three programs that might be useful as antidotes. <u>First</u> is the dormitory counseling—perhaps one counselor for every 35–50 students so that these students can really become close with that counselor and develop a friendship that merits confidence. <u>Second,</u> a professional counseling division would be helpful where students could get vocational, academic, and personal guidance. <u>And finally,</u> a psychiatric division is practically essential where professional services for serious problems may be provided. These are all part of Indiana University's preventive program—and according to Dr. Frederick Coons, the university president, we have had only one suicide since 1955.[5]

The underlined words function as transitions. Numerous transition words, expressions, and phrases exist and are used by speakers to help listeners follow their arguments. Here is a partial list of some of the more commonly used transition words and phrases:

> On the one hand
> On the other hand
> Nevertheless
> In spite of
> Although
> Moreover
> In short
> In sum
> Therefore
> Consequently
> All in all
> In addition
> On the whole
> To sum up
> First, second, third
> Finally
> But

Use these transitional expressions, and others like them, to make your paragraphs flow smoothly.

Express similar ideas in parallel structures

Grammatically parallel structures can be used to underscore the similarity between ideas. A parallel structure simply phrases equivalent items in a similar way. Here is an example of a sentence rewritten so as *not* to be parallel. Notice how awkward it sounds:

> Let every nation know, whether it wishes us well or ill, that we shall pay any price, bear any burden, any hardship will be met, support any friend, oppose any foe to assure the survival and the success of liberty.

The speaker gives a catalog of sacrifices the United States will make "to assure the survival . . . of liberty." Since the catalog expresses a series of equivalent ideas, all its items should be similarly phrased. The underlined entry does not begin, like the others, with a verb, and is therefore not parallel. Here is the sentence as it appeared in the speech:

> Let every nation know, whether it wishes us well or ill, that we shall pay any price, bear any burden, meet any hardship, support any friend, oppose any foe to assure the survival and the success of liberty.[6]

Here is another, more commonplace, example:

Awkward: Clearing the land, hiring the laborers, and the supervision of the architects are all part of the developer's job.

The underlined entry, unlike the others, does not begin with a gerund, and the sentence is consequently not parallel.

Better: Clearing the land, hiring the laborers, and supervising the architects are all part of the developer's job.

Build repetition into your oral paragraphs

Because of the invisibility of the spoken word, oral paragraphs must be more repetitious than written paragraphs. Speakers have to enunciate carefully and repetitiously or they run the risk of being misunderstood. Propositions are stated and restated; complex notions are elaborated on; crucial statements are repeated. Numerous examples of repetition in oral paragraphs can be found:

> We can never be satisfied as long as our bodies, heavy with the fatigue of travel, cannot gain lodging in the motels of the highways and the hotels of the cities. We cannot be satisfied as long as the Negro's basic mobility is from a smaller ghetto to a larger one.
>
> We can never be satisfied as long as our children are stripped of their selfhood and robbed of their dignity by signs stating "for whites only." We cannot be satisfied as long as a Negro in Mississippi cannot vote and a Negro in New York believes he has nothing for which to vote. No, we are not satisfied, and we will not be satisfied until justice rolls down like waters and righteousness like a mighty stream.[7]

Repetition is primarily used in the oral paragraphs of longer speeches. In constructing your own oral paragraphs, use repetition, with moderation, to explain any complex ideas or to emphasize any crucial issue.

Build redundancy into your oral paragraphs

Redundancy—sometimes called "wordiness"—occurs whenever a speaker, either for emphasis or clarity, deliberately overstates a condition, proposition, or idea. In writing, redundancy is a cardinal sin most often committed by the inexperienced. But in oral paragraphs, again because of the invisibility of the spoken word, speakers are often usefully and necessarily redundant. Here is an example:

> Others will debate the controversial issues, national and international, which divide men's minds. But serene, calm, aloof, you

> stand as the nation's war guardians, as its lifeguard from the
> raging tides of international conflict, as its gladiator in the arena
> of battle. For a century-and-a-half you have defended, guarded,
> and protected its hallowed traditions of liberty and freedom, of
> right and justice.[8]

The underlined expressions and words can surely be considered unnecessary in a strict rhetorical sense. Nevertheless, the redundancy of
the paragraph dramatically adds to its impact, if not to its literal
meaning.

Redundancy is a subtle device that should be used with caution.
Paragraphs bloated with synonyms are often tedious to listen to and
difficult to understand. Nevertheless, bearing in mind that your audience can only hear your words, you should phrase your ideas as
redundantly as necessary to make them clear.

Make your paragraphs emphatic

Emphasis is achieved by the expression of more important ideas
in main, or independent, clauses, and of less important ideas in subordinate, or dependent, clauses. In other words, an utterance that is
properly emphatic will rank ideas through grammatical structure. Here
is a simple example of an unemphatic utterance made emphatic
through subordination:

Unemphatic: The doctors fought to save her life. She herself was
brave and spirited to the end. The tumor eventually
killed her.

Emphatic: Although the doctors fought to save her life and she
herself was brave and spirited to the end, the tumor
eventually killed her.

The second construction assigns a main clause to the most important
idea, "the tumor eventually killed her," and a subordinate clause to
the less important ideas, "Although . . . the end." By this grammatical structuring, the relative importance of each idea is made clear.

Skilled speakers habitually word their speeches in such a way as
to make thir principal ideas more emphatic. Consider, for instance,
the following two examples—the first, unemphatic and the second,
emphatic:

> The state of Mississippi swelters with the heat of injustice. The state of Mississippi swelters with the heat of oppression. I have a dream. One day even the state of Mississippi will be transformed into an oasis of freedom and justice.

> I have a dream that one day, even the state of Mississippi, a state sweltering with the heat of injustice, sweltering with the heat of oppression, will be transformed into an oasis of freedom and justice.[9]

A speaker may also achieve emphasis by repeating the key term in a paragraph. In the example below, the famed trial lawyer Clarence Darrow emphatically declares his disbelief in *prophecy* by using singular and plural forms of the word six times in a short paragraph.

> As to prophecies, intelligent writers gave them up long ago. In all prophecies, facts are made to suit the prophecy, or the prophecy was made after the facts, or the events have no relation to prophecies. Weird and strange and unreasonable interpretations are used to explain simple statements, that a prophecy may be claimed.[10]

Repetition of a mechanical and thudding sort can easily be carried too far. But done with moderation and common sense, the repetition of key words within a paragraph can make an assertion more emphatic.

Special kinds of oral paragraphs

Our discussion has so far centered on the informational oral paragraph—that is, the paragraph structured to provide a listener with material that clarifies, amplifies, and documents a generalization. Various other kinds of oral paragraphs perform other functions and are structured differently. Among these are the following.

The introductory oral paragraph   The structure and content of the introductory oral paragraph varies with the purpose and length

of the speech. In short speeches, the primary function of the introductory paragraph is to state the central idea.

*Central
idea:*   Many people have made their expressed purpose in life that of
either proving or disproving the existence of God by the use of
scientific data. Let me point out immediately that what I'm going
to do today is neither of these. What I'm going to try to show is
that man's scientific arguments, by which I mean arguments
drawn from any natural phenomenon, cannot possibly prove or
disprove the existence of God.[11]

Note that the paragraph is not structured to have a generalization
that is then documented by supporting details. Its function is not to
document a generalization but to introduce a central idea.

In longer speeches, the introductory oral paragraph is used to
establish friendly contact between the audience and speaker. The
speaker will either say how happy he or she is to be there or will find
some other means of establishing rapport with the audience.

It is a pleasure to be in Denver once more, to visit again this
university where I taught one happy summer, and to have the
opportunity to renew so many long standing and precious
friendships. Actually, I tend, in retrospect, to associate this insti-
tution with one of the major changes in the direction of my life.
It was here that I enjoyed my last full-time teaching—though I
did not know it at the time—because immediately after my return
from that pleasant summer here I was invited to become the
Provost of Columbia, a decision that, once made, brought my
teaching days to a close. Now that I am here again, who knows
but that when I get back to New York there might be a strong
campus opinion developed in my absence in favor of my return
to teaching. If this should be the case, then I think I ought to
come back here and start where I left off in 1949.[12]

This paragraph obviously has little to do with the proposed topic
of the speech, except to establish a relationship between the speaker
and the audience. Various other openings can be used to gain the
attention and goodwill of an audience, and these are widely practiced
in longer speeches. The point is that introductory paragraphs per-

form a special function and are consequently structured differently from informational paragraphs.

The transitional oral paragraph   Transitional oral paragraphs, as the name implies, are used to move the speech from one major point to another. Generally, they are short paragraphs containing only a sentence or two. Here is a typical example:

> This, of course, is not quite like the notion of some physical diseases. One can have many degrees of arthritis. But one either *has* malaria or does not have it. The same is true with many other diseases. But in the case of mental illness, it seems that any of us can—indeed, all of us *do*—have some degree of it, at some time.
>
> That is my first observation. Now for a second observation.
>
> The general notion has long prevailed that, once mental illness has appeared, the victim is doomed. The illness progresses, the disability increases, the specter of dementia looms inevitably ahead. . . .[13]

The second paragraph is obviously there to ease the transition from one major point to another. Usually, after the transitional paragraph, the speaker will pause before proceeding with added emphasis to the opening sentence of the next oral paragraph.

The concluding oral paragraph   Concluding oral paragraphs often contain sweeping summaries of notions that the body of the speech has sought to prove. Here are two examples:

> There must be no state church and no required religion. But good religion supports legitimate government, and good government is on the side of ethical religion.[14]

> When we understand that these two major stumbling blocks to the educational progress of the underprivileged children can be eliminated—that they can be encouraged to communicate and that apathy and antagonism can be conquered—we realize that we need not write these children off as a lost cause. We need

> not lose these valuable human resources. We can help the "un-teachables" to discover the magic of learning and achieving. We can help them to understand Schulz's definition: "Happiness is finding out you're not so dumb after all."[15]

If the speech is an exhortation, its final paragraph will often appeal to the audience for help. Here, for instance, is the final paragraph from a speech on hemophilia delivered by a hemophiliac:

> I cannot change that part of my life which is past. I cannot change my hemophilia. Therefore I must ask you to help those hemophiliacs that need help. For I remember too well my older brother Herbert, so shattered in adolescence by hemophilia that his tombstone reads like a blessing: "May 10, 1927–April 26, 1950, Thy Will Be Done." And I ask you to help hemophiliacs because one day my grandson may need your blood. . . .[16]

The content of the final paragraph will vary with the purpose and the content of the speech. Moreover, this paragraph—as the last in the speech—will often consist of an appeal to the audience, a summary of the points covered in the speech, or a statement of what good results can be expected if the speaker's recommendations are followed.

Review of applications

The quality of a paragraph, whether oral or written, will ultimately depend on the quality of its details. However, once you have gathered your details together, you must develop them into arresting oral paragraphs. Doing so requires that you (1) develop a single idea in each paragraph; (2) word the generalization in the paragraph to interpret the supporting detail; (3) avoid mixed constructions; (4) use pronouns that refer to unmistakable antecedents; (5) use transitional expressions to link your ideas; (6) express similar ideas in parallel structures; and (7) build repetition, redundancy, and emphasis into your paragraphs. In addition to the kinds of oral paragraphs most often used to convey information to an audience, there are oral paragraphs that are used to introduce a subject, to make a transition between topics, or to conclude a speech. These special paragraphs have a structure of their own and ordinarily do not resemble the paragraph consisting of a generalization and supporting details.

III. CAUTIONS

In writing paragraphs for your speech, one fact should outweigh all others in your mind: that a speech is an oral form. Its message is communicated through the spoken word, which must be instantly understandable to listeners, not readers. You cannot, therefore, sit down and compose the paragraphs for your speech in the way you would normally write out paragraphs for an essay. Most of us, when we write out paragraphs intended to be read, do not read them aloud to ourselves. We have little or no idea what they would sound like out of a speaker's mouth. Nor is it especially important that we should. These paragraphs are, after all, intended merely to be read.

But the paragraphs of your speech are not meant to be read; they are meant to be heard. If you intend to write out your speech, you must compose its paragraphs in a way that will give them the characteristics of orality. One way to do this is to read all your paragraphs aloud to yourself several times. Read them in the way that you intend to speak them. Revise them until you feel comfortable saying them. In short, you must be sure that the paragraphs of your speech are oral paragraphs, not written ones. (For information on the use of words in a speech, see Chapter 10, "Wording the Speech.")

One final caution: Many beginning speakers overlook the fact that an audience cannot see the paragraphs of a speech. In writing, the paragraph is signaled by indentation; in a speech, the paragraph should be signaled not only by transition words but also by a pause. So when you are through with a paragraph, pause for a moment or two before you go on to the next one. By pausing at the end of a paragraph, you let listeners know that you are done with one idea and are about to move on to another. The pause will help you collect your wits and remind yourself—with a glance at your outline—of where you have to go; it will also give the audience a few seconds to reflect on what you have said so far.

Review of cautions

As you write out your speech, bear in mind that its paragraphs are not meant to be read but to be heard. Read each paragraph out loud in the tone of voice you intend to use when you make the speech. Then revise each paragraph until you are satisfied with the way it sounds. Remember, also, that even if you write out your speech in advance, you must not merely read it to the audience. Finally, use a pause to signal the end of one paragraph and the start of another.

EXERCISES

1. Identify the generalizations in the following paragraphs:

   a. In testimony before the same Senate committee, Newark Airport officials reported that as early as 1946 the number of hours in which visibility was cut to six miles or less by smoke alone, or in combination with other factors, totaled 4,359 hours that year—nearly 50% of the total hours during the year. On some occasions air pollutants alone were even sufficient to ground planes at Idlewild airport. In reviewing accident cases for 1962, the Civil Aeronautics Board listed six cases in which obstruction of view due to air pollution was the primary cause. On this basis, since 1960, 50 aeronautical accidents may well have been due to atmospheric pollution. Thus, air pollution fulfills another role on the criminal roster—that of crippler, maimer, and indiscriminate killer in automobile and air accidents.
      —Charles Schalliol, "The Strangler," Indiana Oratorical Association Contest, Bloomington, Indiana, 1967.

   b. Although each case is different, what are some of the general motives for suicide? College psychiatrists, deans, and heads of counseling list several. One would be our search for identity—this has to do with breaking away from home and becoming an adult. Every parent knows that some day his child is going to become an adult. Some parents help their children to accept St. Paul's admonition to "put away childish things." Others don't. As a result, students frequently find themselves being pushed out of their homes, where they have been children, into a college situation where they must be adults.
      —Patricia Ann Hayes, "Madame Butterfly and the Collegian," Indiana Oratorical Association Contest, Bloomington, Indiana, 1967.

    c. There has been a deterioration in the literary style of speeches. Politicians, lawyers, and ministers, the ranks from which most of our speakers are drawn, live in a busy and hurried age; they have less and less time for reading, reflection, and the maturing of their own literary styles; they do not read the masters and the classics as they once did. They are readers of newspapers and periodicals in an age when newspapers and periodicals are less literary and more journalistic. Practitioners of the art of public speaking today are apt to piece together a speech from newspaper clippings and current editorials. Or worse still, the busy public man, engrossed with a thousand and one duties and increasingly dependent upon experts in technical fields for the intellectual materials covering his job, calls upon numerous ghost writers to prepare his speeches. Paragraphs from many sources are then assembled and fitted into the speech.

    —William G. Carleton, "Effective Speech in a Democracy," Southern Speech Association, April 1951.

2. The following paragraphs do not develop a single point but stray from it to some other issue. Identify and excise the extraneous sentences.

    a. Primitive and even civilized people have grown so accustomed to believing in miracles that they often attribute the simplest manifestations of nature to agencies of which they know nothing. They do this when the belief is utterly inconsistent with knowledge and logic. Aristotle, as everyone here knows, was the supreme logician of all times. The deductive syllogism, which Francis Bacon heaped such contumely upon, and unfairly, I might add, nevertheless served mankind as the staple process for reasoning for over a thousand years. In spite of Aristotle and Bacon and the army of logicians before and after, people still remain superstitious. They believe in old miracles and new ones. Preachers pray for rain, knowing fully well that no such prayer was ever answered. When a politician is sick, they pray for God to cure him, and the politician invariably dies. The modern clergyman who prays for rain and for the health of the politician is no more intelligent in this matter than the primitive man who saw a separate miracle in the rising and setting of the sun, in the birth of an individual, in the growth of a plant, in the stroke of lightning, in the flood, in every manifestation of nature and life.

b. Darwin's principle of natural selection, based as it is on constant pressure of competition or struggle, has been invoked to justify various policies in human affairs. For instance, it was used, especially by politicians in late Victorian England, to justify the principles of *laissez-faire* and free competition in business and economic affairs. If Germany had not so over-extended herself simultaneously on two fronts, there is no telling how the Second World War might have ended. The greatest blunder the Germans made was to launch their attack on Russia so late. And it was used, especially by German writers and politicians from the late nineteenth century onwards, to justify militarism. War, so ran this particular version of the argument, is the form which is taken by natural selection and the struggle for existence in the affairs of the nations. Without war, the heroic virtues degenerate; without war, no nation can possibly become great or successful.

3. Rewrite the following sentences to make them parallel.

a. She needs its warm sweetness before the night is out to escape her fears, her guilt, and the remorse she feels.

b. They sold their house, their furniture, and the boat they owned.

c. Patience, diligence, and paying painstaking attention to detail—these are the requirements.

d. As the shoreline lives, decays, and is devoured by itself, it gives birth to numerous, lovely creatures.

e. It is harder to hate people as a whole than hating one's neighbor.

NOTES

[1] Ralph Zimmerman, "Mingled Blood," Interstate Oratorical Contest, 1955.

[2] Mary Katherine Wayman, "The Unmentionable Diseases," Indiana University, Bloomington, Indiana, Summer 1967.

[3] Wayman, "The Unmentionable Diseases."

[4] Gerald Lynch, "The Pursuit of Security," Commencement Speech, University of Dayton, Dayton, Ohio, 1963.

[5] Patricia Ann Hayes, "Madame Butterfly and the Collegian," Interstate Oratorical Association contest, Bloomington, Indiana, 1967.

[6] John F. Kennedy, Inaugural Address, Washington, D.C., 20 January 1961.

[7] Martin Luther King, Jr., "I Have a Dream," Washington, D.C., August 1963.

[8] Douglas MacArthur, "Farewell to the Cadets," West Point, New York, 12 April 1962.

[9] King, "I Have a Dream."

[10] Clarence Darrow, "Why I Am an Agnostic," symposium on religion, Columbus, Ohio, 1929.

[11] Leon R. Zeller, "What Can We Prove About God?" Pennsylvania State University, University Park, Pennsylvania, 1965.

[12] Grayson Kirk, "Responsibilities of the Educated Man," University of Denver, Denver, Colorado, 1964.

[13] Karl Menninger, "Healthier Than Healthy," New York City, 5 April 1958.

[14] Howard C. Wilkinson, "How Separate Should Government and God Be?" Charlotte Executive Club, Charlotte, North Carolina, 1963.

[15] Carolyn Kay Geiman, "Are They Really Unteachable?" University of Kansas, Lawrence, Kansas, 1964.

[16] Zimmerman, "Mingled Blood."

10

Wording the speech

I. PRINCIPLES

Words stand for things, objects, and ideas. When children first learn to talk, they are carefully taught the names of things by their parents. "Dog" says the parent, pointing to the family poodle. "Dog?" queries the child, looking a little mystified. Eventually, through this kind of repetition, the child learns that the word *dog* stands for the familiar four-legged creature.

Without reflection, the advantage of this sort of naming is little appreciated. Words allow us to miniaturize the objects and items in our universe and to carry them conveniently around in our heads. We can sit at a cafe and talk about bulldozers, parrots, and pyramids without either a bulldozer, a parrot, or a pyramid being anywhere near in sight. Most people carry around a great number of words in their heads. Journalists regularly use a vocabulary of about twenty-thousand words; doctors, lawyers, and clerics use about ten thousand words; skilled workers use a vocabulary of nearly five thousand words. Sciences and the learned professions have their own specialized vocabularies, which the person on the street rarely ever hears. Medicine, for instance, has names for some 433 muscles, 193 veins, 707 arteries, 500 pigments, 295 poisons, 109 tumors, 700 tests, 200 diseases, and some 3,000 bacteria. Through words the wisdom of one age is stored and passed on to another.

Abstract and concrete words

Semanticists classify words into two large groups: abstract words and concrete words. Abstract words represent conditions, ideas, notions, and concepts. Words such as *love, hate, liberty* represent states of being and are therefore classified as abstract. Concrete words, on the other hand, stand for tangible, visible objects. The word *apple* is concrete because it represents an object that can be seen and pointed to. Of these two kinds of words, abstract words are obviously the more likely to be misunderstood.

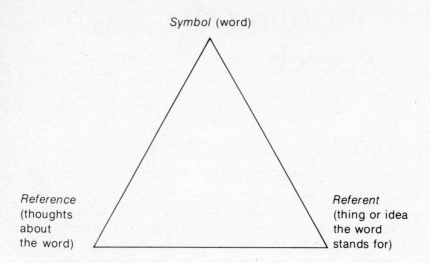

The extent of the misunderstanding possible is evident from this diagram, known as a *semantic triangle.* According to the semantic triangle, the meaning of a word is divisible into two parts: its *reference* and its *referent.* The *referent* of a word is the person, object, or idea that the word represents. For instance, the referent of the word *apple* is obviously the fruit we know by that name. On the other hand, the referent of the word *love* is the heart-palpitating, palm-sweating condition that men and women all over the world occasionally claim to suffer. Dictionaries catalog the common referents of words and can be consulted to settle any disagreements over the literal meaning of a word.

Disagreements over *references,* however, cannot be settled by a dictionary. For references are the thoughts and emotions that different words evoke from different people. At the top of the next page is a semantic triangle showing how the word *marriage* might appear

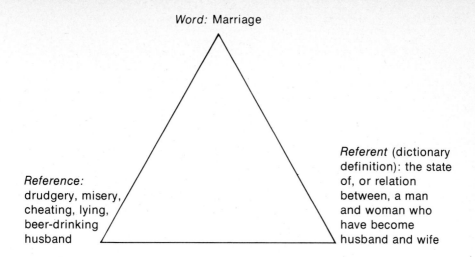

Word: Marriage

Reference:
drudgery, misery,
cheating, lying,
beer-drinking
husband

Referent (dictionary
definition): the state
of, or relation
between, a man
and woman who
have become
husband and wife

to a recently and bitterly divorced woman. On the other hand, at the bottom of the page is how the word *marriage* might appear to a happily married man.

Negative references might also exist for a concrete word. For instance, a man who has once nearly choked to death on an apple is

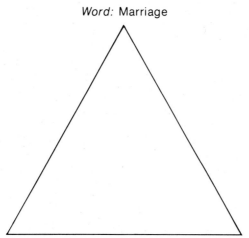

Word: Marriage

Reference:
bliss, connubial
happiness, sharing,
loving partnership

Referent (dictionary
definition): the state
of, or relation between,
a man and woman who
have become husband
and wife

not likely to respond to the word *apple* as benignly as the woman who has eaten hundreds of apples with no ill effects. Nor, for that matter, is the survivor of a shark attack likely to regard the word *shark* in the same way as the person who has only seen a shark on a movie screen. All of us have accumulated personal experiences that cause us to react uniquely to words.

The semantic triangle should teach you two lessons about word usage. The first lesson is that abstract words crucial to the ideas of a speech should be carefully defined. The more abstract the word, the fuzzier the referent, and the greater the chance of misunderstanding. For instance, if you were giving a speech on "The Function of Love in Family Life," you had better begin by making it clear what you mean by *love*—a word so abstract that it is not even uniformly defined in dictionaries. A concrete word such as *hot dog,* on the other hand, need not be defined, since it is not likely to be misunderstood.

The second lesson taught by the semantic triangle is that the dictionary definition of a word is not always an accurate gauge of how an audience is likely to react to it. If individuals can have different references for the same words, so can groups. *Socialized medicine,* used before separate audiences of the chronically ill and of prosperous physicians, will have vastly different references. The word *abortion* may provoke one reaction from an audience of feminists and quite another from an audience of Catholic clergy. In sum, while you will never be able to foretell exactly how an audience might react to your words, you should nevertheless consider the make-up of the audience in wording the speech and try to choose words that will neither provoke, alienate, nor offend.

Denotations and connotations

The *denotation* of a word is the object, idea, or event with which the word can be exactly matched. *Pig,* for instance, denotes the specific animal known by that name. *Love* denotes a specific emotional state. *Turkey* denotes a particular bird, and *tiger* denotes a particular kind of predatory cat. Denotative meaning is therefore nothing more nor less than the exact referent of a word.

But words mean more than they exactly denote. Words reflect the characteristics of their referents as secondary meanings. The turkey, for instance, is an ungainly, stupid bird, given to hideous gobbling and pointless strutting. The turkey is so stupid that it is rather an easy prey. When you call someone a "turkey," you don't mean to say that the person gobbles, struts, and is ungainly; you mean to say that the person is stupid and easily duped. This kind of implied meaning is known as *connotation*.

Skillful writers and speakers use words to denote and connote. Sports announcers connotatively use synonyms for the word *beat* to vary their reports of one team's victory over another. Consider, for instance, the connotative differences in these synonyms for *beat:*

John Q. University *beat* Alfred & William College

downed	whipped
nipped	thrashed
upset	drubbed
clobbered	kayoed
outlasted	pummeled
overcame	edged out
put away	ruined
defeated	destroyed

Finally, notice the skillful use of connotation in this oral paragraph, taken from Bartolomeo Vanzetti's "Last Speech to the Court." Vanzetti, who along with Nicola Sacco was executed for murder on August 23, 1927, is describing and praising his friend, Sacco:

> I have talk a great deal of myself but I even forgot to name Sacco. Sacco too is a worker from his boyhood, a skilled worker lover of work, with a good job and pay, a good and lovely wife, two beautiful children and a neat little home at the verge of a wood, near a brook. Sacco is a heart, a faith, a character, a man; a man lover of nature and of mankind. A man who gave all, who sacrifice all to the cause of Liberty and to his love for mankind; money, rest, mundane ambitions, his own wife, his children, himself and his own life. Sacco has never dreamt to steal, never to assassinate. He and I have never brought a morsel of bread to our mouths, from our childhood to today—which has not been gained by the sweat of our brows. Never.

The same thing could have been said less connotatively, but with less sparkle. For instance, instead of saying, "He and I have never brought a morsel of bread to our mouths, from our childhood to today—which has not been gained by the sweat of our brows," the less sensitive speaker might have made the less connotative and more matter-of-fact assertion: "He and I always worked hard for a living—and never got anything for nothing."

Review of principles

Words are representational; they stand for things, objects, and ideas. Semanticists classify words into two groups: abstract words and concrete words. Abstract words stand for states of being, ideas, conditions, concepts. Concrete words stand for tangible, visible objects. According to the semantic triangle, words have *referents*—the person, object, or idea a word stands for—and *references*—the feelings the word evokes. Since the references of words will vary from group to group, speakers have to choose their words carefully before different audiences. Finally, words also have denotations and connotations. The denotation of a word is its literal meaning, whereas the connotation is its symbolic overtones.

II. APPLICATIONS

Perhaps there was a time when writers wrote like speakers talked. If so, that time is long gone. Many writers nowadays write with all the force and complexity that come from having words mummified on a page. Some monster sentences on the page have gone beyond 4,000 words. *Absalom, Absalom,* a novel by William Faulkner, has a sentence of 1,300 words. The *Guinness Book of World Records* lists a record sentence containing 4,284 words that appeared in the *Report of the President of Columbia University, 1942–1943.* Listeners would surely walk away rather than endure such a barrage.

There are compelling reasons why speakers should compose their sentences altogether differently from writers, and throughout this book we have enumerated many of them. The chief reason, however, is simply this: Listeners cannot understand propositions that are worded in long, complex sentences. Readers can pause to track a wayward verb back to its subject, painstakingly stitch clauses together, and leisurely reconstruct the muddled sentences of a writer. But listeners have neither the time nor the opportunity to do this sort of reconstruction. If listeners fail to get a speaker's meaning on first hearing, the meaning is altogether lost to them.

Some written sentences border on the unintelligible no matter how often they are reread. The traditional sentence style of banks and other business institutions is monstrously complex and impossible to fathom. Many banks have lately recognized that their contracts are incomprehensible to the world at large and have begun to rewrite them. Here, for instance, is a passage from the old loan contract of a bank. Just for fun, read it aloud to a classmate:

> In the event of default in the payment of this or any other Obligation or the performance or observance of any term or covenant contained herein or in any note or other contract or agreement evidencing or relating to any Obligation or any Collateral on the Borrower's part to be performed or observed; or the undersigned Borrower shall die; or any of the undersigned become insolvent or make an assignment for the benefit of creditors; or a petition shall be filed by or against any of the undersigned under any provision of the Bankruptcy Act; or any money, securities or property of the undersigned now or hereafter on deposit with or in possession or under the control of the Bank shall be attached or become subject to distraint proceedings or any order or process of any court.

What does it all mean? Here is the same provision as stated in the new loan contract:

> I'll be in default:
> 1. If I don't pay an installment on time; or
> 2. If any other creditor tries by legal process to take any money of mine in your possession.

The second version contains the sentence style that students should studiously aim for. This style can be achieved if the following guidelines are observed.

Use concrete words

Abstractness of words   Words vary in abstractness. Consider, for instance, if you wanted to talk about the work of the poet Shelley. Below are a number of words, arranged from the most abstract to the most concrete, which could be used to describe Shelley's work. "Shelley's writing" is more abstract than "Shelley's poetry," "Shelley's poetry" is more abstract than "Shelley's sonnets," and "Shelley's *Ozymandias*" is the most specific of all, since it is the name of a particular sonnet by Shelley.

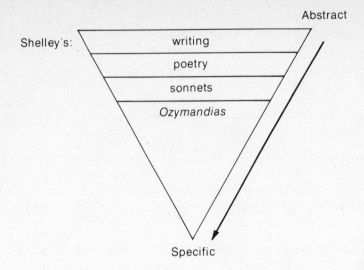

Depending on the words a speaker uses, a topic may be discussed in varying degrees of abstractness. The vocabulary of student speakers, as a matter of fact, tends to be abstract rather than specific. Consider, for instance, this oral paragraph from a student speech:

> Cigarette smoke contains many harmful substances including known cancer agents. These substances affect many parts of the respiratory system. Elements in cigarette smoke affect the cilia—the small waving hairs lining the bronchial tubes—which are responsible for clearing the respiratory system of foreign matter. Moreover, things found in cigarette smoke are deposited in many parts of the body, where they accumulate.

The underlined words and phrases are abstract and vague enough to make the entire paragraph sound fuzzy. Here is a rewrite that replaces the underlined expressions with more concrete words:

> Cigarette smoke contains gases, uncondensed vapors, and liquid particulates, including the chemical benzo(a)pyrene, the deadliest known cancer agent. Gases, such as carbon monoxide, formaldehyde, and hydrogen cyanide, found in cigarette smoke, paralyze the cilia—the small waving hairs lining the bronchial tubes—which are responsible for clearing the respiratory system

of bacteria and particulates. Moreover, particles found in cigarette smoke are deposited in the larynx, carina, major bronchi,
smaller bronchi, bronchioles, and pulmonary tissue, where they
accumulate.

Below are two columns, one listing the abstract word or phrase
used in the first version of the oral paragraph, the other listing the
more concrete replacement that was used in the second version.

Abstract	*Concrete*
many harmful substances	gases, uncondensed vapors, and liquid particulates
known cancer agents	the chemical benzo(a)pyrene, the deadliest known cancer agent
These substances	Gases, such as carbon monozide, formaldehyde, and hydrogen cyanide
affect	paralyze
foreign matter	bacteria and particulates
things	particles
many parts of the body	larynx, carina, major bronchi, smaller bronchi, bronchioles, and pulmonary tissue.

The more concrete you are, the more authoritative and expert your
speech will sound. Nothings hints of amateurishness more quickly
than the use of vague, abstract references and terms.

Use oral words

Speakers should use words somewhat like poets do. Poets—whose
language style is primarily oral—have consistently chosen words for
their sounds as well as for their meanings. For instance, it is a commonsense observation that long, multisyllable words, since they take
longer to pronounce, tend to slow down a line. Consequently, a poet
wishing to create a mood of languorous slowness will often achieve
this effect by deliberately packing long words in a sentence. Consider, for instance, these two lines by Alfred, Lord Tennyson:

> The moan of doves in immemorial elms,
> And murmuring of innumerable bees.

Words can also be chosen to deliberately quicken the tempo of a line, as in this example from a poem by John Milton:

> Swift as the sparkle of a glancing star.

The considerations involved in choosing words for a speech are different from those involved in choosing words for a poem. The poet wishes to reinforce meaning with sound; the speaker wishes to be *instantly intelligible*. Words chosen for a speech should be concrete, familiar, and easily pronounced, otherwise a speaker is likely to end up saying a proverbial "mouthful." Short, simple words, while being easier to pronounce, are also easier for an audience to hear and instantly understand. Here is a passage written to be read rather than spoken. Notice how ponderous and wooden its words sound when read aloud:

> Objective consideration of contemporary phenomena compels the conclusion that success or failure in competitive activities exhibits no tendency to be commensurate with innate capacity, but that a considerable element of the unpredictable must invariably be taken into account.

Here is the same general idea, worded in an oral style, and taken from the most oral of books, the Bible:

> I returned and saw under the sun, that the race is not to the swift, nor the battle to the strong, neither yet bread to the wise, nor yet riches to men of understanding, nor yet favor to men of skill; but time and chance happeneth to them all.

Aside from mouthing unintelligible nonsense, the speaker who uses long, difficult-to-pronounce words in a speech also runs the risk of sounding harsh and cacophonous. Cacophony occurs when words are uttered in a combination that makes an unpleasant and grating sound. Writers, though their words will be read silently by different readers, worry less about cacophony, since it is more difficult to detect on the page than in the utterance. Here is an example of a cacophonous sentence:

> Blatant mistakes of gargantuan dimensions characterize this report.

Read aloud, the sentence seems made up of firecracker syllables that pop and explode in the speaker's mouth. As you practice your speech, cacophonous sentences such as this should become obvious.

Cacophony is not the only sound effect you need to be wary of in wording your speech. You should also be alert to peculiar word combinations that might produce an internal rhyme. Even the loftiest idea sounds silly when stated in a rhyming sentence. The following sentence, from a BBC broadcast, is inadvertently worded to contain internal rhymes:

> The enemy is re<u>ported</u> to have seized this im<u>portant</u> <u>port</u>, and reinforcements are hurrying up in sup<u>port</u>.

Unintentional alliteration—where initial consonants of words sound alike—can also make a sentence sound ludicrous:

> Perhaps his puny profits pose no persistently serious problem.

Alliteration and rhymes, though appropriate sound effects in a poem, do not belong in a speech, unless used intentionally for a burlesque effect.

Use short and moderately short sentences

Long sentences are difficult for listeners to follow and hard for speakers to say. The information in a long sentence is often divided on the page by commas, dashes, and brackets. Punctuation marks, of course, are invisible to listeners and, in a speech, must be signaled by the speaker's voice. It is asking too much of listeners to expect them to follow a long sentence as well as a complex series of punctuation marks heard only through oral clues. Consider this sentence, taken from a biography of Geoffrey Chaucer:

> Even in a fairly large city like London—a mere town by comparison to modern London, though swarming with people packed together in small apartments like chickens in market crates—most people lived out their lives in neighborhoods, tannery workers associating primarily with tannery workers (and the hawkers or stallkeepers who sold them their fruit and vegetables, their pots and pans and the makings for their brooms), wine people associating mostly with wine people, rich men associating mostly with rich men, who attended the same parties or lodged next door, safe in the more comfortable sections of their specialized business districts, in great, sober houses to which the successful, with their servants and apprentices, fled from the noise, stink, and crowding of the poor. . . .

Even Solomon would find this sentence impossible to follow if it was given in a speech.

Very much the same thing could be said in shorter sentences, and with greatly improved clarity. This is how a speaker could put the same ideas:

> By comparison to modern London, London was then a mere town. But even in such a large city, people lived with people, packed together in small apartments like chickens in market crates. Most people lived out their lives in neighborhoods. Tannery workers associated with tannery workers and with the hawkers or stallkeepers from whom they bought their fruits and vegetables, their pots and pans and the makings for their brooms. Wine people associated mostly with wine people. Rich men associated mostly with rich men, who attended the same parties or lodged next door. The rich lived safe in the more comfortable sections of their specialized business districts. They occupied great, sober houses, to which they fled with their servants and apprentices to avoid the noise, stink, and crowding of the poor. . . .

The point is not to talk in short, childish sentences, like characters from some absurdist play, but to talk in sentences varied enough to be interesting yet short enough to be instantly understood.

Keep subjects close to verbs

If subjects and verbs are kept close together, the intelligibility of sentences is vastly increased. Ordinarily, when we talk, we tend to naturally keep our subjects close to their verbs.

1. John went to town.

2. The *Titanic* was a large ship of wonderful proportions.

3. Smoke paralyzes the cilia and causes them to stop beating.

The underlined words are subjects and verbs. Notice that in every case the one follows closely behind the other, making for instantly intelligible constructions.

Under the pressure of the moment, however, many speakers tend to become parenthetical. Clauses, phrases, and appositives are wantonly inserted between subject and verb, creating a dislocation in the natural subject-verb order and making the sentence more difficult to understand.

1. John, who wore a frayed winter coat and who last year suffered a severe case of frostbite in a December blizzard, went to town.

2. The *Titanic,* fantastically conceived, beautifully engineered, magnificently decorated, was a ship of wonderful proportions.

3. Smoke, which leaves the burning zone of the cigarette at 884°C, paralyzes the cilia and causes them to stop beating.

If you read these three sentences aloud, you will quickly see how much more difficult they are to understand than the first three, where subjects and verbs are kept close together. These same ideas could have been more intelligibly put, if they had been stated as separate sentences:

1. John went to town, wearing a frayed winter coat. Last year, he suffered a severe case of frostbite in a December blizzard.

2. The *Titanic* was fantastically conceived, beautifully engineered, and magnificently decorated. She was a ship of wonderful proportions.

3. Smoke leaves the burning zone of the cigarette at 884°C. It paralyzes the cilia and causes them to stop beating.

Use short and simple subjects

Sociologists and bureaucrats are fond of constructing sentences with serpentine subjects. These subjects are generally hammered out of a succession of nouns and noun phrases.

> <u>The implementation of the Safety at Sea Act that followed the sinking of the *Titanic*</u> required all ships to carry enough lifeboats for their passengers.

The underlined words make up the subject of the sentence. Substitution by a pronoun—the standard test for identifying a subject—is possible:

> <u>It</u> required all ships to carry enough lifeboats for their passengers.

What required?

> The implementation of the Safety at Sea Act that followed the sinking of the *Titanic*

This kind of construction, with a long, complex subject, is tediously difficult to understand. Listeners must hang giddily onto the subject as it slowly unravels, then quickly attach it to its verb. It is better to have two sentences:

> Following the sinking of the *Titanic,* the Safety at Sea Act was implemented. This act required all ships to carry enough lifeboats for their passengers.

Use the active voice

Speakers use the active voice almost instinctively. It is far commoner for a speaker to say:

> I vividly remember my last trip to England.

than to say:

> My last trip to England is vividly remembered by me.

Under certain conditions, writing the passive voice is justified. Scientific papers, for instance, are usually written in the passive voice to invest their findings with a kind of subjectless universality. Speakers, however, are better off using the active voice. Sentences in the active voice—the more familiar oral construction—are easier to understand; moreover, sentences in the active voice sound friendlier and less pompous. Instead of saying something like:

> A number of geophysical and biological processes are known in which carbon monoxide is produced.

say:

> A number of known geophysical and biological processes produce carbon monoxide.

In sum, when composing a speech, you should draft sentences that are easy to say. Read the sentences out loud. If they don't sound like something you would naturally say, rewrite them until they do. Remember that oral sentences should be more casual and informal than sentences that are written for an essay or term paper. Prepositions should occur at the end of the sentence, if that's where they would naturally go. Don't say, "This is the sort of work for which he was fitted." Instead, say "This is the sort of work he was fitted for." Use contractions like "don't," "aren't," and "won't" even if you wouldn't use them in writing. Avoid stilted and literary phrases such as "It must be borne in mind," or "With reference to." Address your audience as "you." Finally, bear these numbers in mind, courtesy of readibility expert Rudolf Flesch, who says that a seventeen-word sentence is standard; a twenty-one-word sentence is fairly difficult; a twenty-five-word sentence is difficult; and a twenty-nine or more word sentence is very difficult. Though they refer to the readability of sentences, these figures nevertheless can give you an idea of how difficult your sentences might be to a listener.

Review of applications

Because listeners must get a speaker's meaning the first time, speakers should compose their sentences altogether differently from the way writers do. Primarily, you should aim for an oral style in you speech—a style that is easily comprehensible on first hearing. You can achieve this style by using words that are both oral and concrete; by using short or moderately short sentences; by keeping subjects close to verbs; by using short and simple subjects; and by using mainly the active voice in your sentences.

III. CAUTIONS

Never silently draft a speech; always read it aloud during the writing and rewriting. Let your ear dictate your revisions. Often it is only in reading the speech aloud that you can detect the wooden-sounding passage or the pompous phrase or word. Bear in mind, as you write the speech, that you must choose your words not only for what they mean to you but for what they are likely to mean to your particular audience (see Chapter 4). Wording that works effectively with one audience may alienate or confuse another.

There are, moreover, some specific stylistic cautions that a speechwriter should observe.

Beware of big words

English has an immense vocabulary. It contains numerous abstract words that have an impressive and dignified ring but are vague to the point of meaninglessness. The repeated use of these words create gobbledygook—talk or writing that sounds pompous, wordy, and silly. To illustrate how the overuse of abstract words creates gobbledygook, we reproduce below the "Bafflegab Thesaurus," which originated from a Royal Canadian Air Force listing of fuzzy words. Any word from column A, matched with any word from columns B and C, will produce abstract, yet lofty-sounding, nonsense.

	A	B	C
1.	integrated	management	options
2.	total	organizational	flexibility
3.	systematized	monitored	capability
4.	parallel	reciprocal	mobility
5.	functional	digital	programming
6.	responsive	logistical	concept
7.	optional	transitional	time-phase
8.	synchronized	incremental	projection
9.	compatible	third-generation	hardware
10.	balanced	policy	contingency

Do not be deluded into thinking that the bigger and more abstract the words, the more moving and impressive a speech is likely to sound. Wondrously grave statements have been made with short, simple words. Here is a striking example of the power of short, familiar words:

> I am tired of fighting. Our chiefs are killed. Looking Glass is dead. Toohulsote is dead. The old men are all dead. It is the young who say no and yes. He who led the young men is dead. It is cold and we have no blankets. The little children are freezing to death. My people, some of them, have run away to the hills and have no blankets, no food. No one knows where they are—perhaps they are freezing to death. I want to have time to look for my children and see how many of them I can find. Maybe I shall find them among the dead. Hear me, my chiefs, I am tired. My heart is sad and sick. From where the sun now stands I will fight no more forever.[1]

Don't accumulate initial clauses

Sentences that bristle with initial clauses are more often found in writing than in speeches. Such sentences are easy to read but difficult to listen to. Here is an example:

Awkward: His use of drums, his use of horns where before only violins dared to venture, his swelling, flashy rolls of the piano, his bold, almost brassy renderings of themes— these were the distinctive stamps of genius that characterized the music of Beethoven.

It is possible for listeners to follow such utterances, but only with great patience and care. Better to state the same ideas more plainly:

Better: Beethoven's music bore distinctive stamps of genius. His use of drums and horns was wholly original. His music was characterized by swelling, flashy rolls of the piano, and bold, almost brassy renderings of themes.

Don't use inverted sentences

Writers sometimes invert the parts of a sentence either for emphasis, variety, or some other effect. Such constructions, while they may be stylish and eye-catching on the page, are difficult for listeners to understand. Here is an example:

Awkward: That smoking causes lung cancer, coronary artery diseases, chronic bronchitis, and emphysema was the irrefutable finding of the Surgeon General.

Speakers would not utter such a sentence naturally. Here is the same sentence, but in normal word order:

Better: The irrefutable findings of the Surgeon General were that smoking causes lung cancer, coronary artery diseases, chronic bronchitis, and emphysema.

Generally speaking, you are better off avoiding such inverted constructions in speech. If you feel compelled to invert an occasional sentence, invert only short sentences, and only for emphasis. Instead of saying:

>The *Titanic* went down to her watery grave.

you could say:

>Down to her watery grave went the *Titanic*.

Review of cautions

Since a speech is meant to be heard rather than read, your ear should dictate its wording. The diction of the speech should also be adapted to your particular audience. Specific stylistic cautions include warnings against the use of big words, the accumulation of initial clauses in a sentence, and the use of inverted sentences in the speech.

EXERCISES

1. Pick out the more concrete word from the following pairs of words:

expenses	Pisces	Geronimo
food bills	astrological signs	Indian
ulcer	dictionary	paper
sickness	book	foolscap

prisons	sailboats	biplanes
institutions	ketch	airplanes
science	short story	bird
chemistry	fiction	sparrow

2. Correct any word usage problems you find in the following sentences:

   a. The pallid pallbearer poked his head into the parlor.

   b. The *Titanic* was a gigantic ship.

   c. He asked us to follow into the hollow of the hills.

   d. Sloppy, slatternly speech often characterizes their exchanges.

3. From the following pairs of words, choose the one whose connotative meaning fits better with the rest of the sentence:

   a. The lame beggar (hobbled, sauntered) through the doorway.

   b. She gave a wicked smile and cocked her eyebrows in an expression of arch (enjoyment, amusement).

   c. His contemptuous attitude has (buffaloed, alienated) many of his friends.

   d. Grieving, the widow and her children made their way (ponderously, solemnly) through the cemetery.

   e. He told her wicked lies, adding (contrivance, deception) to his other offenses.

4. Rewrite the following sentences to make them easier for listeners to understand:

   a. Howard Richards, whose book *They Shall Inherit the Earth* is a damning indictment of the carelessness with which our most esteemed institutions have administered their public trust, was of a contrary opinion.

   b. The administration of the cafeteria finances by the Central Student Committee has resulted in many unnecessary expenses.

   c. John Chaucer was "a citizen of London," as he was proud to say, a rich and influential vintner—which is roughly the fourteenth-century equivalent of the modern large brewer in Ireland or England, though John Chaucer was not by any means a personage up to the enormous wealth and power of, say, the Busch family of St. Louis or the greater beermeisters of Germany, men more nearly comparable with fourteenth-century barons.

d. That the city council is derelict of its duty, that it should be subjected to an immediate recall vote, is evident from its dismal failure to find an answer to the sewer problem.

e. While the FDA is responsible for the purity of our food, the efficacy and safety of our drugs, and the hygienic standards of food processors, it is not responsible for running our private lives.

NOTES

[1] Chief Joseph of the Nez Perce Tribe, "Surrender Speech."

11

Practicing speech delivery

I. PRINCIPLES

"To slur is human," said John Mason Brown. Many of us not only slur, we mumble, chew our words, or spit them out like seeds. Some of us talk through our noses; some of us swallow our words. "Americans," according to one speech authority, "are best known for having the worst articulation in the Western world."[1]

The principal aim of all speech is intelligibility. We talk not just to be heard, but to be understood. Intelligibility is a variable quality. Some speakers are clear, crisp, and instantly understandable; others slur their words, mumble, or talk too fast to be intelligible. Still other speakers cannot articulate certain sounds. The cartoon character Elmer Fudd, for instance, missays his *r*'s as *w*'s—a speech characteristic shared by newscaster Barbara Walters.

What do listeners deduce about a speaker from his or her voice? They deduce a surprising amount of information, although some of it is of dubious accuracy. Studies have found that listeners tend to judge the status and credibility of a speaker from the speaker's voice.[2] Use a flat tone of voice, and listeners will consider you cold and withdrawn; use a nasal tone, and they will find you repugnant. Speak in a high-pitched voice, and you'll be judged as effeminate; speak at a rapid rate, and you'll be seen as enthusiastic.[3] Indeed, the way you talk has an effect even on your employability, especially if you are looking for a clerical or technical position.[4] "There is no index of character so sure as the human voice," said British statesman Benjamin Disraeli. Apparently many people believe that.

The psychology of speech delivery

Students in speech classes are often unsure about how they should behave when they give speeches. Some play the "orator"; others play the "anti-orator." One student in giving a middling speech on "The Lamaze Method of Natural Childbirth" got up to the podium, squared her shoulders, and looked her audience straight in the face. Giving the back row a broad wink, she puffed herself up and began declaiming as though she were an evangelist speaking to throngs in the Astrodome. When she was done, she repeated the wink to the back row, drawing a titter, and resumed her seat.

A second student behaved in exactly the opposite way—playing the part of the "anti-orator." He slouched to the podium, stared morosely at his shoe, and began to mumble. The students in the back row protested that they couldn't hear him. He raised his voice, stared defiantly at the students, and continued with the speech. As soon as he was done, he scampered back to his seat, breathing a loud sigh of relief.

Giving a speech before a classroom of their peers causes student speakers varying degrees of discomfort. All classes require students to produce, but usually in private transactions involving only the student and teacher. English classes require students to write papers; chemistry classes require students to do experiments. But neither the papers nor the experiments are ever seen by anyone other than the teacher. In speech classes, however, students are required to produce visibly and publicly—to get up before both students and teacher and give a speech.

Although in-class speechmaking may initially cause you to be uncomfortable, perhaps it would help if you knew more or less what teachers and audiences expect from student speeches. First of all, most teachers expect students to give speeches but not to playact at doing them. The ideal is to speak and behave as if you're holding an extended conversation with yourself. Speak loudly enough to be heard, casually enough to be pleasant, and naturally enough to be yourself. Don't put on airs or puff yourself up with oratorical self-importance. Emphasize your points with gestures, but not to a silly excess.

Second, most teachers—as well as most educated audiences—prefer content to posturing, reason to hysterics, and logic to claptrap.

The vast majority of teachers are rather kindly disposed toward student speeches and are about as forgiving of errors as you would be of the conversational manners of a friend. You needn't, therefore, try to be especially dramatic or rousing in your delivery. Instead, if you manage to be audible, reasonable, and intelligible, your speech will most likely be a success.

Finally, teachers do not expect students to adopt a special language or delivery style just for the purpose of giving a speech. Good delivery is neither cute nor noticeable. Like tact, good delivery is a trait whose presence is never detected, but whose absence is glaringly obvious. Preserve your own way of talking when you give a speech (that is, of course, so long as your natural manner of speaking is understandable). Retain your own characteristic gestures; use the same pauses and emphases in the speech as you would in a one-to-one conversation. Rather than acting the part of someone else as you deliver the speech, you should concentrate on serving up a heightened form of the real "you."

Review of principles

Intelligibility should be the principal aim of every speaker. But a speaker's voice often conveys more to an audience than simply information on the speech topic. Frequently, an audience will make inferences about the credibility and status of a speaker from the sound of the speaker's voice. While students often have mistaken ideas about how they should behave in delivering their speeches, most teachers merely expect student speeches to be delivered in a voice that is both audible and intelligible. You should also try to deliver the speech in a natural voice and not attempt to strike an oratorical pose.

II. APPLICATIONS

"The sound must seem an echo to the sense," wrote the English poet Alexander Pope. He was referring to the use of rhyme and rhythm in poetry. Pope's maxim also applies to speech delivery. Adjustments must be made in delivery, depending on the speech occasion. It is inconceivable, for instance, that a speaker would use the same style of delivery at a wake as at a wedding. Some variables of delivery are adjustable on demand; others are not. For example, you cannot drastically alter the quality of your voice to suit every occasion. But you can talk either softer or louder, slow down the rate of your speech, and use fewer gestures. In sum, it is possible to modify your delivery to match the occasion for speechmaking.

Appropriateness is the cardinal rule to be observed in making adjustments in speech delivery. To paraphrase Pope, "The delivery must seem an echo to the sense." Or, to put it more prosaically, the delivery style must be appropriate to the content and occasion of the speech. It is simply a matter of common sense—the same sort of common sense you would use in deciding how to recite a poem. These lines, for instance:

> Rats!
> They fought the dogs and killed the cats,
> And bit the babies in the cradles,
> And ate the cheeses out of the vats,
> And licked the soups from the cooks' own ladles,
> Split open kegs of salted sprats,
> Made nests inside men's Sunday hats,
> And even spoiled the women's chats,
> By drowning their speaking
> With shrieking and squeaking
> In fifty different sharps and flats.
> —Robert Browning,
> *The Pied Piper of Hamlin*

obviously cry out for a different recital style than these lines:

> Break, break, break,
> On thy cold gray stones, O Sea!
> And I would that my tongue could utter
> The thoughts that arise in me.
> —Alfred, Lord Tennyson,
> *Break, Break, Break*

The differences in these stanzas call for obvious delivery and interpretative adjustments in a reciter. Differing occasions of speechmaking likewise require speakers to adjust their styles of delivery.

In addition to the adjustments you might have to make because of the occasion and subject of a particular speech, with every speech you should practice some elementary rules of delivery.

Speak loud enough to be heard

Volume—the loudness of sound—is measured in decibels. A whisper from about four feet away measures 20 decibels; faint speech occurs at about 40 decibels; an ordinary conversation from a distance of three feet takes place at between 55 and 66 decibels.

Whether or not a speaker is talking loud enough to be heard depends upon at least two factors. The first is the amount of background noise. The background noise of an empty theatre is about 25 decibels; of the average home, about 32 decibels; of a noisy restaurant, about 70 decibels. To be understood in these environments, speakers must talk above the decibel level of the background noise.

The distance of a listener from the speaker is a second factor affecting whether or not the speaker can be heard. Imagine that there are five rows of toy boats floating in a bathtub and that a pebble is tossed in front of the first row. Waves from the pebble will cause the first row of boats to bob vigorously up and down, the second less so, the third even less, and the fifth least of all. Sound waves have a similar effect on rows of listeners. The waves diminish in intensity as they ripple away from their source. Listeners in the row nearest to the speaker receive the sound waves in greatest intensity; listeners farther away receive them in least intensity and consequently do not hear the speaker as clearly.

Volume is a prime factor in a speaker's intelligibility. If you don't talk loud enough, listeners will neither hear you nor understand you. Bear in mind that your own voice, because it is amplified by the bones of your skull, sounds louder to you than to a listener. To be sure you're talking loud enough, look at listeners in the back row. If you see them craning forward, cupping their hands to their ears, or looking disgruntled and bored, you're probably not talking loud enough.

Articulate your words properly

Articulation is the sound-producing process by which we utter clear, distinct syllables. Students generally confuse articulation with pronunciation. Some dictionaries, in fact, list the two words as synonyms. But articulation and pronunciation refer to different aspects of the speechmaking process. Pronunciation is the way that individual words should be uttered. For instance, the correct pronunciation of the word "fable" is listed in *Webster's New World Dictionary* this way: fā′b′l. The vowel *a* is elongated; the *e* at the end of the word is silent. Articulation refers to the manner in which speakers say vowels and consonants. Some speakers chronically slur their words, blithely ignoring the dictionary guide to pronunciation. Other speakers are unrepentant clippers who snip syllables off every word they utter. In sum, pronunciation refers to the way individual words should be spoken; articulation refers to the way individual speakers say various words. Here in an imaginary exchange between two fishermen is articulation at its very worst:

When Fishermen Meet

Hyamac.	Lobuddy.
Binearlong?	Coplours.
Cetchenenny?	Goddafew.
Kinarthy?	Bassencarp.
Enysiztoom?	Coplapounds.
Hittenhard?	Sordalike.
Fishinonabodem?	Rytonabodem.
Watchaadrinkin?	Jugojimbeam.
Igoddago.	Tubad.
Seeyaroun.	Yetekedezy.
Guluk.	

Poor articulation is a prime cause of speaker unintelligibility. The more distinctly you utter your vowels and consonants, the easier you are to understand. The more you mumble, clip, snip, slur, or chew your words, the less intelligible you become. Some speakers have articulation problems caused by a speech defect. But for the majority of healthy mumblers, poor articulation is caused by bad speech habits. Most of us mumble and gobble our words in casual talks with our friends; our friends likewise return the favor by mumbling and gobbling to us. We are as benignly forgiving of their articulation as they are of ours. Gobbling and mumbling, in fact, constitute a kind of speech norm when friends casually meet. But it is a corrupting norm that, if not counteracted by exposure to more formal speech occasions requiring distinct articulation, will quickly infect our way of speaking. Chronic articulation problems—even a bad case of slurring—are not easily overcome. If you don't articulate well, consult with your teacher. Various articulatory exercises exist, which, if conscientiously practiced, can help the slurrer.

Speak at an understandable rate

Rate is the speed at which a speaker talks. Normal rate of speech varies from between 140 to 180 words per minute, depending on whether a speaker is calm, tense, angry, or agitated. When we are angry or excited, we tend to speak faster; when we are depressed or subdued, we tend to speak at a slower rate.

Rate of speech has an obvious and immediate effect on a speaker's intelligibility. Some speakers talk at a dizzying rate, reeling off words and sentences in an unintelligible jumble. Student speakers, especially when they are suffering from speechfright, are often guilty of talking too fast. The contrary mistake—of talking too slowly—is rarer but just as likely to affect intelligibility. Listeners who must wait an interminable time for a speaker to complete a sentence are likely to stop listening and start daydreaming. Cowpokes may sound romantic when they drawl, but slow-talking speakers soon begin to seem merely boring.

Vary your pitch for emphasis

Pitch refers to the relative highness or lowness of sounds. Different sounds are heard at a different pitch. The buzz of a bee, for instance, is heard at a lower pitch, while the squeak of a mouse is heard at a higher pitch. Sounds differ in pitch because sound waves differ in frequencies. The thirty thousand nerve fibers in the inner ear are stimulated by, and tuned to detect, sounds of different frequencies that are heard at a different pitch. Audiologists measure hearing on a scale that ranges from a low to a high pitch. Hearing loss can occur at one end of the scale without affecting a person's ability to hear sounds at the other.

The customary pitch at which a person generally speaks is said to be the *key* of his or her voice. Men generally speak at a lower pitch than women. A study indicated that a higher pitch in a man's voice is generally perceived as a sign of either a dynamic, feminine, or artistically inclined personality. Women who speak at a higher pitch are perceived by their listeners as dynamic and extroverted.[5]

No skilled speaker would address an audience in a monotone—with no change in voice inflection or pitch. We all have a pitch range,

which we use to emotionally color our utterances. Consider, for instance, the word *you* spoken with various pitch inflections.   ↗ u
                                                                          Y o

said with a rapidly rising pitch, implies a different emotion (Is it really you!) than Y ＼ spoken with a falling pitch (Not you, again!)
                    0
                      u↘

The first *you* indicates pleasure, excitement, and surprise at seeing someone; the second *you* implies displeasure and disappointment. The same word spoken as a flat monotone Y o u⃗ expresses a third reaction (Oh, it's only you). Speakers modulate pitch to animate their words and sentences and to imply something of how they feel. Pitch change for emotional coloring, however, is seldom premeditatedly done except by actors plying their craft. We don't pause in midsentence and meditate on what pitch to use on the next word. Instead, most of us change pitch naturally and unconsciously, depending on how we feel at the moment.

Speaking oral paragraphs

A written paragraph is identified on the page by a visible indentation; an oral paragraph is identified by the way it is spoken. Listeners have no other clues to the procession of oral paragraphs except in the enunciation emphases provided by a speaker's voice. Oral paragraphs should therefore be spoken as separate units of thought in the speech, much as a reciter would speak the different stanzas of a poem. Below are some guidelines to help you speak coherent and understandable oral paragraphs.

Pause at the end of an oral paragraph   Listeners have no way of knowing when a paragraph has ended unless you so indicate with a pause. The pause allows listeners to digest what has just been said and to anticipate what is about to come. Moreover, it signals to them the end of one idea and the introduction of another.

Emphasize the generalization of the oral paragraph   Such emphasis is achieved through proper enunciation of the generalization—the single most important idea of the paragraph—and the idea that the paragraph should amplify and develop. If listeners mishear the generalization of a paragraph, the supporting details will be meaningless to them.

Emphasize transition from one paragraph to another   Following the pause that signals the end of a paragraph, you should emphasize any transitional words or phrases such as *moreover, however, but, nevertheless,* which signal the movement of the speech from one paragraph to another. With this sort of emphasis provided, listeners will be better able to track the development of a speech through a succession of oral paragraphs.

Finally, in delivering the speech you should not resort to a predictable or singsong way of emphasizing its oral paragraphs. Use gestures and variations in volume, rate, and pitch to emphasize the movement of the speech from one paragraph to another. But don't successively use the same gestures and the same variations, or your speech will sound as though it were being delivered by a robot.

Review of applications

Appropriateness to the content and the occasion is the cardinal rule of speech delivery. You must adjust your delivery according to your reason for giving the speech, its topic, and your audience. In addition, you should speak loud enough to be heard; properly articulate your words; speak at an understandable rate; and use pitch to convey emphasis. In speaking oral paragraphs, you should pause at the end of each paragraph and emphasize its generalization. You should also highlight the transitions that move your speech from one paragraph to another.

III. CAUTIONS

As you begin practicing your speech, bear in mind a simple truth: mental rehearsal is no rehearsal at all. It does no good to read the speech silently to yourself while imagining that you are delivering it. To get any benefit from rehearsing, you must practice out loud, preferably to a friend or to anyone who is willing to listen and react to both delivery and content. This is the only way for you to see what effect your words are likely to have on an audience. Moreover, practicing out loud will let you know whether your speech really has an oral style.

A useful way to judge your speech is either to hear or to watch yourself make it. Through the use of audio or video tape, it is now possible to do exactly that. If you can, we recommend that you make a tape of your speech. Taping the speech will allow you to see or hear yourself as a listener would. Some departments have video-taping equipment available for student use, and if yours does, by all means use the equipment in your rehearsing.

Finally, you should never rehearse gestures. If you do, your delivery will inevitably appear as if it were "packaged." Don't worry about what you'll do with your hands during the speech. When it's your turn to speak, simply do what seems most natural. What you are after is a delivery style that seems unaffected and spontaneous, not one based on oratorical posturing.

Review of cautions

Mental rehearsal is no rehearsal at all. To be useful, your rehearsals must be out loud and, if possible, before a listener. If you can, make either an audio or a video tape of your speech, to see how you look and sound to a listener. Finally, you should never rehearse gestures. When the time comes to make the speech, use your hands in whatever way seems most natural.

NOTES

[1] William Norwood Brigance, *Speech: Its Techniques and Disciplines in a Free Society* (New York: Appleton-Century-Crofts, 1961).

[2] L. S. Harms, "Listener Judgments of Status Cues in Speech," *Quarterly Journal of Speech* (April 1961), pp. 164–168.

[3] David W. Addington, "The Relationship of Selected Vocal Characteristics to Personality Perception," *Speech Monographs* 35 (November 1968):492–503.

[4] Robert Hopper and Frederick Williams, "Speech Characteristics and Employability," *Speech Monographs* 40 (November 1973):296–302.

[5] Addington, "The Relationship of Selected Vocal Characteristics," p. 502.

12

Revising the speech

I. PRINCIPLES

Throughout this text, we have repeatedly emphasized the differences between the language styles of writers and speakers. We have pointed out that, for the most part, an oral paragraph is more repetitious than a written paragraph, an oral sentence is more instantly intelligible than a written sentence, and an oral vocabulary is more colloquial than a written vocabulary. "Does it read well?" remarked British parliamentarian Charles Fox. "Then it's not a good speech." No doubt his was an exaggerated and biased view. Some good speeches do read well; some do not. But all good speeches appeal as much to the ear as to the eye.

Because of the differences between writing and speaking, a speech should be revised not only on the page but, principally, in the utterance. You should tinker with the speech only after enunciating it out loud. Ask a friend to be your critic by sitting in the back row, listening to your speech, and making suggestions about improving it. If you cannot get a friend to help you, use a tape or video recorder to monitor the way your speech sounds. In sum, make all revisions on the basis of how the speech sounds when given out loud, not on how it reads on the page.

Basically, what you are after in revising the speech is a good oral style—one, to borrow somewhat from the British author W. Somerset Maugham (1874–1965), that is characterized by these three qualities: lucidity, simplicity, and euphony. First, the style of the speech should be lucid; that is, the speaker's ideas should be clear and understandable. Second, the speech should be simple: not necessarily simple in its ideas, but as simple as possible in its expression of them. Third, the style of the speech should be euphonious. Its words and phrases should be both easy to say and easy to hear. As you revise the speech, pay attention not only to what your words mean but also to how they sound.

Review of principles

Writers and speakers usually have different language styles. Because of this difference, you should revise your speech not on the page but in the utterance. As you revise, give your language a good oral style—one characterized by lucidity, simplicity, and euphony. Your ideas should be clear and expressed as simply as possible; your words should be both easy to say and easy to hear.

II. APPLICATIONS

To help you with the revision of your speech, in this chapter we condense information and advice given in earlier chapters about various parts of the speech. Make your revisions by systematically following the checklist below and going over your speech for the flaws and weaknesses noted under each heading.

Check the structure of the speech

Folk wisdom tells us that some people cannot see the forest for the trees. Indeed, it is a common blunder to become so engrossed in the individual words, sentences, and paragraphs of a speech that you overlook some obvious defect in the structure of the speech itself. Therefore, check both your outline and the text of the speech to be sure that in the heat of composing you didn't stray from the central idea of the speech or deal lopsidedly with its various topics. Here, for instance, is an outline that, if followed, would result in a lopsided treatment of the topics in the central idea:

Central idea: The police have two different roles: the criminal and the noncriminal role.

    I. The criminal role

   II. The noncriminal role
      A. Traffic control
      B. Personal counseling
      C. Providing information

Such structural defects are more easily spotted in an outline than in a speech.

In drafting the speech, it is more than likely that you have deviated somewhat from the outline. If so, make a new outline of the speech as you have written it, and check it for digressions or lopsidedness. Bear in mind that the sequence of topics in the speech should conform to the sequence announced in the central idea. If the central idea promises to deal first with the criminal role of the police and then with the noncriminal role, that is the order of presentation that should be followed in the speech. Consistency of this sort makes the speech easier for an audience to follow. For more discussion on the kinds of structural defects to look for in a speech, review Chapter 8.

Check the wording of the central ideas

Of all the ideas contained in a speech, the central idea should be the most clearly and emphatically worded and the most distinctly enunciated. The central idea is to the speech what a foundation is to a building. Some advice about the central idea is given in Chapter 5, which you should now take time out to review. Be especially certain that the central idea sums up the main contentions of the speech, and that the body of the speech reinforces and develops the main points of the central idea.

Check the wording of the introductory paragraph

Speeches, like chess games, benefit from good openings. Many listeners sound out a speech from its first paragraph and make the decision at that point to snooze or not to snooze. Various openings can be used to jolt awake the would-be snoozers and hold their interest. You could begin with a shocking announcement or remark. Here is a classic example of the use of this tactic:

Henry Ward Beecher had a genius for bringing the most somnolent audience to life. One July morning he rode into a West Virginia town which was widely known in lecture circles as "Death Valley"—for the reason that any speaker unfortunate enough to have an engagement to lecture there wilted and curled up when he faced the town's stupid and indifferent audience.

Beecher was duly warned. That afternoon, when he was being introduced, half the audience was already dozing. Beecher rose from his chair and, wiping his brow with a large handkerchief, strode to the front of the platform.

"It's a God-damned hot day," the clergyman began.

A thousand pairs of eyes goggled and an electrical shock straightened the crowd erect. Beecher paused, and then, raising a finger of solemn reproof, went on, "That's what I heard a man say here this afternoon!"

He then proceeded into a stirring condemnation of blasphemy and, needless to say, took the audience with him.

You could also begin the speech *in medias res* (in the middle of things) like the ancient Greek poets, who always began their epics right in the thick of things—a quarrel, a battle, or some other such stirring event. Here is an example of a speech that opens *in medias res:*

And Allen had of course arrived—as the law required—escorted by one (or both) parent (parents) not as the law required, but as the officer suggested. He had no personal belongings with him, not that they were forbidden—he just didn't have any. He had a coat; he had part of a coat (the rips and tears secured with safety pins and high hopes). And his shoes were worn through and stuffed with cardboard—not that it would matter in there. Even looking at the building frightened him; the bars, the screened-in windows, and locked doors, the people inside he had never seen (but had heard of) who were strict and cold, generous only in the distribution of punishment and the resurrection of easily forgotten rules. The door opened. He went in. And Allen began his first day at school.[1]

It is impossible to give an exact prescription for the kind of opening to use for a speech. It depends on what your speech is about, and what your audience is like. Generally speaking, you should use the opening paragraph to win the audience's interest and to state the central idea. If the opening paragraph of your speech, instead of orienting the audience, immediately begins to smother them with mounds of technical matter, you should rewrite it. Audiences will be more kindly disposed toward you and more manageable when gently led to the heart of a subject.

Check the wording of the oral paragraphs

Ask your listener/friend to give an opinion on each paragraph after you have uttered it. Check the generalization in each paragraph for clarity and force of expression. Be sure that each generalization is adequately developed and amplified by supporting details. To help you, you should review Chapters 7 and 9.

Oral paragraph transitions—within paragraphs and between paragraphs—should be checked. If the speech seems to lurch abruptly from one paragraph to another, you should insert more external transitions between the paragraphs. If the discussion within individual paragraphs seems rough and uneven, more internal transitions are probably needed. You should also check paragraphs for their orality—the ease with which they can be spoken and instantly understood. Bear in mind that oral paragraphs are generally more repetitious and redundant than written paragraphs. If any point within a paragraph seems cryptic or unclear to your listener, use repetition and restatement to clarify it.

Check the diction of the speech

Diction refers to the individual words that make up the speech. Reread Chapter 10, "Wording the Speech," for advice on word usage. Be especially careful about the use of unfamiliar, sesquipedalian words such as *sesquipedalian*—merely another word for very long. Use a colloquial vocabulary—the sort of words and expressions that occur naturally when you're talking. Rewrite any cacophonous combinations or any obvious internal rhymes.

Check the sentence structure of the speech

In the wording of the speech sentences, you should aim for instant intelligibility. Long, involved, twisted sentences should be rewritten to be shorter, more understandable units. Check for awkward placement of verbs and nouns; for overuse of long, cumbersome subjects; for use of complex inverted constructions that are difficult to understand. It is best to check all sentences as you speak them. Ask your friend/listener how any dubious sentence sounds. Ask yourself whether or not you would speak the sentence in conversation with a friend. If the answer is "no," rewrite the sentence.

Check the final paragraph for closure

In his famous poem *The Hollow Men,* T. S. Eliot penned a well-known line about the world ending "not with a bang but a whimper." A similar end threatens many speeches.

As with introductory paragraphs, there are various tactics for constructing final paragraphs, but all final paragraphs should be characterized by *closure*—a sense of having come to a logical and expected end. Some final paragraphs achieve closure by restating or summarizing what has been already said in the body of the speech. Some end by drawing conclusions, or proposing a course of action. Here, for instance, in a satirical speech titled "Advice to Youth," Mark Twain ends by drawing an unexpected conclusion. In the speech, he has dispensed tongue-in-cheek advice to his youthful audience, urging them to obey their parents when the parents are present, to hit disrespectful strangers with a brick, and to lie carefully so as not to get caught.

> But I have said enough. I hope you will treasure up the instructions which I have given you, and make them a guide to your feet and a light to your understanding. Build your character thoughtfully and painstakingly upon these precepts, and by and by, when you have got it built, you will be surprised and gratified to see how nicely and sharply it resembles everybody else's.

In sum, final paragraphs should end with more bang than whimper. State your conclusions; give your suggestions; draw your inferences. Do so positively and forcefully and the speech will seem to naturally and logically come to an end.

Check your delivery for vocal emphasis

Practice and refine your delivery before your friendly listener, experimenting with vocal emphasis until you are satisfied. Remember

to enunciate oral paragraphs as separate units, to mark their beginning and end with pauses, and to duly emphasize their generalizations. For further suggestions on delivery, review Chapter 11.

Once you have practiced the speech and refined your delivery of
it, you can mark cues to yourself on the manuscript. Underlining, for
instance, can be used to indicate vocal emphasis of some sentence or
passage; arrows or other marks can be used to indicate pauses. Cue
yourself on the manuscript with any other delivery instructions.

Finally, though no universal blueprint for revising a speech can
be given other than the general advice of this chapter, students who
try in their revisions to make their speeches clearer and more "talk-
able" cannot go wrong.

Review of applications

We recommend that you follow a systematic checklist in revising
your speech. First, check the structure of the speech to be sure that
no topic is treated in a lopsided way. Then check the wording of the
central idea and the introductory paragraph. After that, check the
diction and sentence structure of the entire speech. Finally, examine
your final paragraph for closure and review your delivery for appropriate vocal emphasis.

III. CAUTIONS

Our primary caution is to urge you to revise with your audience
firmly in mind. Remember that the speech is intended for them, not
for some unknown critic. If you have done your homework on your
audience, you should have some definite ideas about what is likely to
appeal to them and what is not. Whether or not the speech as it
stands will get through to a particular audience is, within limits, the
criterion you should use in all your writing and revising (see Chapter
4).

Be sure, too, that your efforts at revising are directed at both the
small and large elements of the speech. You should not only change
individual words and phrases that don't sound right; you should also
be willing to restructure or completely rewrite whole paragraphs. If
some supporting detail seems fuzzy, be prepared to replace it. Also,
be sure that the overall emphasis in the speech is on the significant,
rather than the trivial, aspects of your subject.

Review of cautions

You should revise the speech with your audience firmly in mind. Make your changes based on what you think will appeal to them. Be sure, also, that you revise both the large and small elements in the speech—whole paragraphs as well as individual words. And make sure that the focus of the speech is on the significant points of your subject.

NOTES

[1] Patricia Warren, "Bring Forth the Children," Interstate Oratorical Association Contest, 1971.

GENERAL TYPES
OF SPEECHES

13

The speech to inform

I. PRINCIPLES

What is the informative speech? Basically, it is a speech whose primary purpose is to give information. We say primary because in speechmaking, as in most kinds of human activities, purity of purpose is a rarity. The informative speech principally intends to inform; but in the act of informing, it might also persuade or even entertain. Such effects, however, would be secondary to its primary purpose.

Speeches of this kind cover a vast number of topics, since even the simplest subject can usually be explained in a more detailed and informative way. The speech to inform can carry us through specific instructions, describe far-off cities and sights, explain ordinary or complex events. It can tell us how the bullfighter kills a bull, how a department store computes finance charges, or how we can change our names. Such speeches usually answer the simple interrogatives: who, what, when, where, how, or why.

We have emphasized before that all speeches should be directed to a specific audience in a specific way, and the speech to inform is no exception to this principle. There are at least two fundamental conditions that this type of speech must satisfy. First, it must tell the audience what they do not already know about the topic; second, it must tell the audience what they implicitly or explicitly need to know.

For instance, the sample speech included in this chapter (pages 193–95) contains a wealth of information about botulism that an audience of college freshmen would not be likely to know. Its concluding paragraph explains how botulism can be avoided. In sum, the speech to inform should have a *raison d'être*—a reason for being. Audiences will not sit through a speech crammed with generalities about a subject; nor will they endure a speech about some esoteric topic far removed from their needs, wants, and desires.

Review of principles

Although purity of purpose is rare even in speechmaking, the speech to inform aims principally at imparting information to an audience. To be successful, such speeches must provide an audience with information they don't already have and which they either implicitly or explicitly need.

II. APPLICATIONS

The molecule of any speech is the oral paragraph. The speech to inform is usually made up of oral paragraphs that narrate, define, describe, divide and classify, compare and contrast, explain process, and analyze cause. Separate paragraphs are ordinarily devoted to each of these functions.

The oral paragraph that narrates

The narrative paragraph is one that tells a story or relates an anecdote. It deals with events and incidents in a definite sequence. Speakers use narratives for a variety of reasons, but an important use is often to make an idea appealing to an audience. Here is an example of that use from Chapter 7:

> I never listen to a speaker launch out on one of those long discussions, filled with statistics of all kinds, or commit the same error myself, but that I think of the professor in a western university who taught mathematics and statistics. One day he was

swimming, dressed in his bathing suit, at the edge of a swimming pool on the university campus when a beautiful coed accidentally dropped her camera into the deep end of the pool. She called to the elderly professor for help. He said he would be glad to dive down after the camera, but first wanted to know why she happened to choose him when there were so many young men within easy reach to do the job. She answered, "Professor, you have apparently forgotten me, but I am in your large statistics class. I have found that you can *go down deeper, stay down longer, and come up drier* than anyone I know"—I do not propose to go down too deep, stay down too long, or come up too dry with these statistics.

The narrative allows the speaker to broach the topic of statistics, which audiences are famous for disliking, with a bit of humor.

Some basic techniques can be identified in all good narrative paragraphs. The first is the use of a consistent point of view. The story is told from one person's point of view—in the case above, the professor's—and this point of view is maintained throughout the paragraph. The language used is consistent with what could be expected of the person from whose point of view the story is told. In this example, the indirect speech attributed to the professor is consistent with the way we expect an elderly professor to sound. On the other hand, if the narrator had made the professor reply to the student by saying, "Hey, you nuts or something? You think I'm going to break my neck diving after your dumb camera?" the inconsistency would have ruined the story.

The second technique practiced in good narrative paragraphs is proper pacing. Pacing refers to the inclusion only of detail that is relevant to the story line and the omission of everything else. In the example above, the narrator mentions only that the professor was swimming at the edge of a swimming pool when he was approached by a beautiful coed. A little reflection tells us that hundreds of details have been purposely omitted—details about the weather, the pool, even the coed. None of this detail would have been relevant to the story, and so the narrator wisely did not use it.

Finally, good narratives make a point. They do not exist for their own sake but usually for the sake of some larger issue. Sometimes they clarify an issue; sometimes they turn a serious issue into a humorous one, or a humorous issue into a serious one. Always, though, they make a point. Here is an example, from a speech, "Advice to Youth, About 1882," by Mark Twain:

> Never handle firearms carelessly. The sorrow and suffering that have been caused through the innocent but heedless handling of firearms by the young! Only four days ago, right in the next farmhouse to the one where I am spending the summer, a grandmother, old and gray and sweet, one of the loveliest spirits in the land, was sitting at her work, when her young grandson crept in and got down an old, battered, rusty gun which had not been touched for many years and was supposed not to be loaded, and pointed it at her, laughing and threatening to shoot. In her fright she ran screaming and pleading toward the door on the other side of the room; but as she passed him he placed the gun almost against her very breast and pulled the trigger! He had supposed it was not loaded. And he was right—it wasn't. So there wasn't any harm done. It is the only case of that kind I ever heard of. Therefore, just the same, don't meddle with old unloaded firearms; they are the most deadly and unerring things that have ever been created by man. . . .

Most narratives start out by telling what their point is, as Twain does in this example; some end by saying what the point is, as does the narrative about the professor. But a narrative must have a point. And it must get to it quickly.

Finally, narratives are widely used as examples, especially in arguments, and often serve as evidence or proof. For example, in a debate over tightening laws against drunken driving, a story about the death of a young man or woman at the hands of a drunk can have a dramatic impact on an audience. Of course, it is misleading to base an argument on one story, but stories can and do add an exemplifying touch to an abstract proposition. And where the story is a dramatic or poignant one that supports the speaker's point of view, it can be immeasurably persuasive.

The oral paragraph that defines

A definition attempts to answer the most basic question an audience can have about an object: What is it? Definitions usually identify the category to which the item belongs and then show how the item differs from others in that category. Here are a few abbreviated examples of definitions:

> Chemistry is the science whose primary concern . . .
> Love is an emotion characterized by . . .
> An atomic clock is a method of keeping time that uses . . .

For the purpose of exemplifying, we have deliberately worded these abridged definitions to rather mechanically link the item to be defined with its category. More subtle and varied wordings are, of course, possible. In our examples, *chemistry* is linked to the category of science, *love* to emotion, and *atomic clocks* to methods of time-keeping. Once identified with a category, the item is then differentiated from others in the same category. Characteristics that differentiate chemistry from other sciences, love from other emotions, and atomic clocks from other methods of timekeeping therefore have to be detailed for the definitions to be complete. Here is an example. First, *palimpsest* is identified with the category of writing surfaces, and then it is differentiated from them:

> Palimpsest is a writing surface, whether of vellum, papyrus, or other material, which has been used twice or more for manuscript purposes. Before the invention of paper, the scarcity of writing material made such substances very valuable and the vellum surfaces were often scraped or rubbed or the papyrus surfaces washed. With material so used a second time it frequently happened that the earlier script either was not completely erased or that, with age, it showed through the new. In this way many documents of very early periods have been preserved for posterity.

Because objects and ideas are often named for their origins and functions, etymologies—explanations that trace the roots and histories of words—are often used in definitions. Here an etymological explanation is used to help define *botulism:*

> What is botulism? Botulism is poisoning caused by the toxin of the bacteria *Clostridium botulinum. Clostridium* is Latin for "little spindle," which is what the bacterium looks like under a microscope; *botulinum* comes from *botulus,* the Latin word for "sausage," the food in which the poison first made its appearance.

Such an explanation not only tells the audience how the organism got its name; it also describes something of the organism's appearance and its history.

Giving examples is another widely used method of defining. Examples can clarify the meaning of a term by citing applications of it. Here, for instance, in two paragraphs, the psychiatrist Carl Rogers defines a technical term, *congruence,* with the aid of examples:

It has been found that personal change is facilitated when the psychotherapist is what *he* is, when in the relationship with his client he is genuine and without "front" or facade, openly being the feelings and attitudes which at the moment are flowing *in* him. We have coined the term "congruence" to try to describe this condition. By this we mean that the feelings the therapist is experiencing are available to him, available to his awareness, and he is able to live these feelings, be them, and able to communicate them if appropriate. No one fully achieves this condition, yet the more the therapist is able to listen acceptantly to what is going on within himself, and the more he is able to be the complexity of his feelings, without fear, the higher the degree of his congruence.

To give a commonplace example, each of us senses this quality in people in a variety of ways. One of the things which offends us about radio and TV commercials is that it is often perfectly evident from the tone of voice that the announcer is "putting on," playing a role, saying something he doesn't feel. This is an example of incongruence. On the other hand each of us knows individuals whom we somehow trust because we sense that they are being what they are, that we are dealing with the person himself, not with a polite or professional front. It is this quality of congruence which we sense which research has found to be associated with successful therapy. The more genuine and congruent the therapist in the relationship, the more probability there is that change in personality in the client will occur.[1]

Testimony from an authority is also frequently used in definitions, especially when the term to be defined is technical or controversial. Here is an example:

What is this thing called hemophilia? Webster defines it as "a tendency, usually hereditary, to profuse bleeding even from slight wounds." Dr. Armand J. Quick, Professor of Biochemistry at Marquette University and recognized world authority on this topic, defines it as "prothrombin consumption of 8 to 13 seconds." Normal time is 15 seconds. Now do you know what hemophilia is?[2]

Although they are found in a wide variety of speeches that have a variety of purposes, definitions are especially useful and necessary in the informative speech.

The oral paragraph that describes

A definition tells; a description shows. Often in giving a speech that informs, it is necessary to both show and tell. Descriptive paragraphs, however, are not effective if they merely contain a catalog of adjectives. The most effective description assembles its adjectives under a *dominant impression*. As the term implies, the dominant impression is a principal characteristic of the thing to be described and forms the hub of the descriptive paragraph. Here are two paragraphs describing hell, taken from a sermon in James Joyce's *Portrait of the Artist As a Young Man*, which exemplify the use of a dominant impression:

> Hell is a strait and dark and foulsmelling prison, an abode of demons and lost souls, filled with fire and smoke. The straitness of this prisonhouse is expressly designed by God to punish those who refused to be bound by His laws. In earthly prisons the poor captive has at least some liberty of movement, were it only within the four walls of his cell or in the gloomy yard of his prison. Not so in hell. There, by reason of the great number of the damned, the prisoners are heaped together in their awful prison, the walls of which are said to be four thousand miles thick; and the damned are so utterly bound and helpless that, as a blessed saint, Saint Anselm, writes in his book on similitudes, they are not even able to remove from the eye a worm that gnaws it.
>
> They lie in exterior darkness. For, remember, the fire of hell gives forth no light. As, at the command of God, the fire of the Babylonian furnace lost its heat but not its light so, at the command of God, the fire of hell, while retaining the intensity of its heat, burns eternally in darkness. It is a never-ending storm of darkness, dark flames and dark smoke of burning brimstone, amid which the bodies are heaped one upon another without even a glimpse of air. Of all the plagues with which the land of the Pharaohs was smitten one plague alone, that of darkness, was called horrible. What name, then, shall we give to the darkness of hell which is to last not for three days alone but for all eternity?

Both paragraphs owe their intensity to the speaker's use of unifying dominant impressions. The first paragraph develops the dominant impression of the straitness—the narrowness—of hell; the second paragraph focuses on the darkness of hell. No doubt hell is more than simply strait and dark; the speaker says it's also noisy and smelly. But he wisely refrains from trying to cover more than a single characteristic of hell in each paragraph. Other paragraphs deal separately with the noise and smell of hell. The result is intense and concentrated description.

Beginning speakers often err in their descriptions by trying to do too much at once. Impressions are jumbled in a hodge-podge mixture of adjectives and adverbs. Sights and sounds are not sorted out and developed in individual paragraphs but are, instead, blended helter-skelter within a single passage. Such descriptions have no impact because they have no central theme. Better, instead, to select a single dominant impression and to build a paragraph around it. Descriptions, after all, cannot do everything, cannot include every conceivable impression, cannot accommodate every sight, sound, smell. Speakers and writers are therefore better off sacrificing completeness in order to achieve intensity.

The oral paragraph that divides and classifies

Imagine that you're giving an informative speech about poetry. Somewhere in the speech you'll have to acquaint the audience with the different kinds of poetry. You might use an oral paragraph, or a series of oral paragraphs, to amplify and develop the following generalization:

> Poetry comes in four principal types: the epic, the lyric, the ballad, and the dramatic monologue.

Such a paragraph—having as its primary purpose the division of a whole into its constituent parts—is said to be based on the principle of division and classification. Entire speeches are sometimes based on such divisions. A speech on "Types of Life Insurance Policies," though intended to inform, would nevertheless be structured on the principle of division and classification. More commonly, division is used as the organizing principle in separate oral paragraphs. Here, for example, are three oral paragraphs based on division:

There are five venereal diseases, all of which can cause death. Three of these have been eliminated by modern medicine, while the other two, syphilis and gonorrhea, are on the rise once more all over the world. Both of these diseases are mainly contracted through sexual relations. These germs spread to all parts of the body, and, therefore, anything the infected person uses is possibly an immediate carrier. These germs can spread to another human by an open cut if it comes in contact with the germs of an infected person.

The symptoms of these diseases are usually disregarded by their victims. In infectious syphilis there are three definite stages, with a few weeks lapsing between the first two. This first stage consists of a hard chancre (SHANK-er) sore in the genital area. The second stage is a rash accompanied by headaches, fever, sore throat, or loss of hair. The third stage, after a seemingly dormant period of 10 to 25 years, makes its presence known by rendering its victim blind, crippled, insane, sterile, or dead.

Unlike its counterpart, gonorrhea's latent stages are more easily noticed by its victims. The first symptom is usually a burning pain during urination. The remaining factors of this disease are similar to those of syphilis, and the results are equally as devastating.[3]

The first paragraph is based on a division of venereal diseases; the second, on a division of the stages of syphilis; the third, on a division of the stages of gonorrhea. Each paragraph is based on a single division, from which the speaker never wanders.

The oral paragraph that compares and contrasts

A comparison attempts to find similarities between two subjects; a contrast attempts to find dissimilarities. Entire speeches are sometimes organized on this principle—of either comparing two things, contrasting them, or doing both in the same speech. Speeches that simultaneously compare and contrast two subjects are, in fact, commoner than speeches that do one or the other exclusively.

Suppose you were giving a speech on this topic: "Hostel or Bed-and-Breakfast Lodging: Which Is Better for the Young American Traveling in Europe?" Implicit in this unwieldy title is your intention to compare the facilities of a bed-and-breakfast lodging with the facilities of a hostel. But it is nearly impossible just to *compare* both, for items of contrast between them are bound to exist. The bread-and-breakfast lodging may be slightly more expensive than the hostel, but it is also likely to be more private and more convenient. Notice how naturally a comparison and contrast begins to evolve. The two topics go together as naturally as the proverbial horse and carriage.

But in separate oral paragraphs it is common to find either straight comparisons or straight contrasts. Here, for instance, is an oral paragraph that simply contrasts:

> Well, a just law is a law that squares with a moral law. It is a law that squares with what which is right, so that any law that uplifts human personality is a just law. Whereas that law which is out of harmony with the moral is a law which does not square with the moral law of the universe. It does not square with the law of God, so for that reason it is unjust and any law that degrades the human personality is an unjust law.[4]

And here is a paragraph that simply compares:

> Whales and human beings are like two nations of individuals who have certain characteristics in common. As mammals they both are warm-blooded, giving milk, and breathing air. As social creatures they both have basic urges for privacy as well as for fraternization. As species bent on reproduction they both show similar patterns of aggression during courtship, the male trying to get the female's attention and the female responding. Finally, as mystical beings they both are caught in the net of life and time, fellow prisoners of the splendor, travail, and secrets of earth.

The contrast and the comparison are each done within a single paragraph. Items to be compared/contrasted are brought together within a single paragraph, and comparison/contrasting remarks made about them.

A comparison or contrast, however, may also be conducted over several paragraphs. Here is an example:

Our Puritan ancestors were preoccupied with sin. They were too preoccupied with it. They were hag-ridden and guilt-ridden and theirs was a repressed and neurotic society. But they had horsepower. They wrested livings from rocky land, built our earliest colleges, started our literature, caused our industrial revolution, and found time in between to fight the Indians, the French and the British, and to bawl for abolition, women suffrage and prison reform, and to experiment with graham crackers and bloomers. They were a tremendous people.

And for all their exaggerated attention to sin, their philosophy rested on a great granite rock. Man was the master of his soul. You didn't have to be bad. You could and should be better. And if you wanted to escape the eternal fires you'd damned well better be.

In recent years all this has changed in America. We have decided that sin is largely imaginary. We have become enamoured with "behavioristic psychology." This holds that man is a product of his heredity and his environment, and his behavior to a large degree is foreordained by both. He is either a product of a happy combination of genes and chromosomes or an unhappy combination. He moves in an environment that will tend to make him good or that will tend to make him evil. He is just a chip tossed helplessly by forces beyond his control and, therefore, not responsible.

Well, the theory that misbehavior can be cured by pulling down tenements and erecting in their places elaborate public housing is not holding water. The crime rates continue to rise along with our outlays for social services. We speak of underprivilege. Yet the young men who swagger up and down the streets, boldly flaunting their gang symbols on their black jackets, are far more blessed in creature comforts, opportunities for advancement, and freedom from drudgery than 90% of the children of the world. We have sown the dragon's teeth of pseudo-scientific sentimentality, and out of the ground has sprung the legion bearing switch-blade knives and bicycle chains.[5]

The first two paragraphs catalog the moral stance of the Puritans, along with their accomplishments; the second two paragraphs contrast the morality and living conditions of modern America with the speaker's rather nostalgic view of the blessed Puritans. Though he argues somewhat glibly, the speaker nevertheless draws an effective contrast over several paragraphs.

The choice of whether a comparison/contrast should be done within or between paragraphs is generally dictated by how complex the comparison/contrast is to be and how complete. If it is to be long, complex, and detailed, obviously it should be done over several paragraphs. If the comparison/contrast is to be short and relatively simple, then a single paragraph will probably do.

Efficient comparison/contrasts are rather simple to do. First, you bring together side-by-side the items to be compared. Next, you decide the bases on which you intend to compare them. Take, for example, the title of the speech given earlier, "Hostel or Bed-and-Breakfast Lodging: Which Is Better for the Young American Traveling in Europe?" In drawing up such a comparison/contrast, many teachers recommend that students simply make up two columns, one for the hostel, the other for the bed-and-breakfast lodging. The bases for the comparison are then listed in the margin and appropriate comparisons/contrasts entered under each column. Here is an example:

	Hostel	*Bed-and-breakfast lodging*
1. *Expense:*	Hostel cheaper.	Bed-and-breakfast lodging is more expensive by about $2 to $3 per night.
2. *Sleeping accommodations:*	Guests sleep in a sex-segregated dorm.	Guests sleep in private rooms.
3. *Bathroom facilities:*	Guests share a common bath room with others in the dorm.	Guests share a bath, usually with one or two other guests.
4. *Food:*	No food is provided. Food can be purchased, usually at a cafeteria.	A home-cooked breakfast comes with the price of the room.
5. *Contact with locals:*	Contact usually restricted to other foreign travelers.	Host or hostess usually friendly and eager to talk about their country. Good means of making contact with locals.

In assembling this comparison/contrast, the speaker needs merely to elaborate on each point, and insert appropriate expressions indicating either comparison or contrast. The following expressions indicate comparison:

> also
> as well as
> bears resemblance to
> like
> likewise
> both . . . and
> in common with
> in like manner
> similar
> too

The following expressions indicate contrast:

> on the contrary
> on the one hand . . . on the other hand
> but
> otherwise
> however
> in contrast to
> in opposition to
> whereas
> still
> unlike
> yet
> although this may be true
> for all that

The comparison/contrast oral paragraph serves many functions in speeches to inform. Speakers construct such paragraphs to help them define, describe, or simply inform their audience about something by contrasting it to what it is not. In constructing such oral paragraphs, you should cover both sides of the issue and use appropriate expressions to indicate either comparison or contrast.

The process oral paragraph

Process oral paragraphs usually answer the interrogative *how*. A process involves a sequence, either of events or of instructions. A paragraph that explains process might, therefore, give instructions on how to bake a cake, might explain the steps one must take to get a bank mortgage, or might catalog the sequence of events that lead to botulism poisoning. In all cases the speaker is required to explain, in proper sequence, how a thing is done, or how an event takes place. Here is a process paragraph explaining how to sharpen a knife:

> The sharpening stone must be fixed in place on the table, so that it will not move around. You can do this by placing a piece of rubber inner tube or a thin piece of foam rubber under it. Or you can tack four strips of wood, if you have a rough worktable, to frame the stone and hold it in place. Put a generous puddle of oil in the stone—this will soon disappear into the surface of the new stone, and you will need to keep adding more oil. Press the knife blade flat against the stone in the puddle of oil, using your index finger. Whichever way the cutting edge of the knife faces is the side of the blade that should get a little more pressure. Move the blade around three or four times in a narrow oval about the size of your fingernail, going *counterclockwise* when the sharp edge is facing right. Now turn the blade over in the same spot on the stone, press hard, and move it around the small oval *clockwise,* with more pressure on the cutting edge that faces left. Repeat the ovals, flipping the blade over six or seven times, and applying lighter pressure to the blade the last two times.

The primary requirements of process oral paragraphs are clarity and a strict observance of proper sequence. Because sequence is more difficult to follow when heard than when read, speakers have to construct their process paragraphs with painstaking care. The process should be explained in minute, understandable steps. Process oral paragraphs should be as short as possible, and should use repetition and transitions to help the audience follow the explanations of the process. Such paragraphs should also be clarified and highlighted by gestures, diagrams, and emphatic delivery.

If the entire speech is organized around the explanation of a process, it is often useful to announce this purpose at the outset and to simultaneously divide the process into stages, which can then be used as headings for various paragraphs. For instance, if you were giving a speech on "How to Find a Job," you might word the central idea as a statement of purpose:

> The purpose of this speech is to tell you how to find a job.

Then you can propose subdivisions of the process:

> Job-hunting, in fact, is easier if applicants do the follow-
> ing: (1) find the hidden job market; (2) locate the hidden
> job openings; and (3) sell themselves to the appropriate
> executive in charge of hiring.

The process has been divided into manageable stages, which can then
be treated separately in different paragraphs. Moreover, to help unify
the speech, the speaker can remind the audience of these major stages
just before amplifying on any one of them. For example, the lead-in
to a new paragraph might remind the audience of the second stage
in finding a job:

> The second step is locating the hidden job openings. How
> are these hidden job openings found?

Such repetition might strike the student as tedious, but it is necessary
to make a process clear.

The oral paragraph that explains cause

Causal analysis—whether in a single paragraph or in an entire
speech—aims at cataloging the causes of some event, or at docu-
menting the results of some condition. Primarily, such an analysis
attempts to answer the interrogative *why*. "Why did the *Titanic* sink?"
"What are the causes of backaches?" "What are the effects of inflation?" These and similar queries, when systematically answered in
either a paragraph or a speech, result in a causal analysis.

Paragraphs structured to explain cause may either plainly announce that purpose or simply imply it. Here, for example, is a paragraph in which the writer makes no bones about what he is about to
do:

> Why have giants vanished from our midst? One must never ne-
> glect the role of accident in history; and accident no doubt plays
> a part here. But too many accidents of the same sort ceases to
> be wholly accidental. One must enquire further. Why should our
> age not only be without great men but even seem actively hostile
> to them? Surely one reason we have so few heroes now is pre-
> cisely that we had so many a generation ago. Greatness is hard

> for common humanity to bear. As Emerson said, "Heroism means difficulty, postponement of praise, postponement of ease, introduction of the world into the private apartment, introduction of eternity into the hours measured by the sitting-room clock." A world of heroes keeps people from living their own lives.
> —Arthur M. Schlesinger, Jr., *The Decline of Heroes*

Plainly, the governing principle behind the structure of this paragraph is to explain cause—to answer its own question, "Why have giants vanished from our midst?" Once the question is answered, the paragraph comes to an end. Other business—further questions, answers, explanations—will be taken up in later paragraphs.

Other paragraphs that explain cause, however, may be more subtle about doing it—to the disadvantage of speaker, reader, and listener. Here, for instance, is a paragraph that attempts to explain the causes of air pollution, but in rather a roundabout way:

> Industry was once considered the major polluting influence of our atmosphere. This is no longer the case. The automobile has become overwhelmingly the most serious problem we face in air pollution control. As the Senate Subcommittee on Air and Water Pollution expresses it, "automotive exhaust is cited as responsible for some 50% of the national air pollution problem." And the problem of automotive fumes shows every sign of becoming more acute. While America currently has 86 million motor vehicles on its streets and highways, the Public Health Service estimates that we will have 120 million internal combustion machines on our highways by 1980.[6]

With some minor rewording, the purpose of this paragraph can be made plainer, and the material becomes easier to follow:

> Industry was once considered the chief cause of atmospheric pollution. But this is no longer the case. The primary cause of air pollution is, without question, the automobile. As the Senate Subcommittee. . . .

All oral paragraphs, but especially oral paragraphs that attempt to explain so abstract a phenomenon as cause, are subject to Murphy's Law—"If anything can go wrong, it will." Indeed, had Murphy been a speaker, he might have coined a special law for the causal oral paragraph, "If anything can be misinterpreted, it will be." Speakers should therefore never try to disguise the organizing principle behind their oral paragraphs. If you intend to present a paragraph that analyzes cause, no harm can come from announcing your intention. Endless misunderstanding, however, can result from your failure to do so.

Some paragraphs, instead of explaining cause, set out to document effect. For instance, a speaker may ask, "What are the effects of a progressive education?" The answer to such a question might result in the second of these two paragraphs:

> We are now at the end of the third decade of the national insanity known as "progressive education." This was the education where everybody passed, where the report cards were non-committal lest the failure be faced with the fact of his failure, where all moved at a snail pace like a transatlantic convoy so that the slowest need not be left behind, and all proceeded toward adulthood in the lockstep of "togetherness." Thus the competition that breeds excellence was to be sacrificed for the benefit of something called "life adjustment."
>
> With what results? We have watched juvenile delinquency climb steadily. We have produced tens of thousands of high school graduates who move their lips as they read and cannot write a coherent paragraph. While our Russian contemporaries, who were supposed to be dedicated to the mass man, have been busy constructing an elite, we have been engaged in the wholesale production of mediocrity. What a switch![7]

The first of these two paragraphs defines progressive education: the second analyzes its effects. If the speaker had asserted that students were delinquent and academically untrained, and then set out to explain why, he would have been analyzing cause.

Paragraphs of mixed purpose

Some paragraphs have one primary purpose—for instance, to define, describe, or analyze cause—which they tenaciously carry out to the exclusion of everything else. The structure of such paragraphs is influenced by their purpose. Comparison/contrast paragraphs, on the one hand, will generally alternate back and forth between the items being compared, using expressions to indicate whether a contrast or comparison is being drawn. Defining paragraphs, on the other hand, will primarily say what a thing is, either through the use of etymological histories, examples, or authority testimony. In either case, the chief purpose of the paragraph determines its structure. However, no rhetorician can classify or anticipate every conceivable paragraph structure. Language is too complex to be made completely subservient to rules. Effective paragraphs of a mixed purpose are written and uttered daily by inventive writers and speakers. Here is one such paragraph:

Definition: { There are few words which are used more loosely than the word "Civilization." What does it mean? It means a society based upon the opinion of civilians. It means that violence, the rule of warriors and despotic chiefs, the conditions of camps and warfare, of riot and tyranny, give place to parliaments where laws are made and independent courts of justice in which over long periods those laws are maintained. That is Civilization—and in its soil grow continually freedom, comfort, and culture. *Analysis of Effect:* { When Civilization reigns in any country, a wider and less harassed life is afforded to the masses of the people. The traditions of the past are cherished, and the inheritance bequeathed to us by former wise or valiant men becomes a rich estate to be enjoyed and used by all.[8]

We bring up the notion of mixed paragraphs to remind you, at the risk of saying the obvious, that language rules are made to be judiciously broken. Writers and speakers should not substitute the conventions of rhetoric for inventiveness. The point in speaking, after all, is to communicate, not to scrupulously practice a body of rules. Clarity and intelligibility should be the primary goals of your communication. The means by which you achieve these goals should be fashioned, not from the observance of rules, but from your own inventiveness.

Constructing the speech to inform

We have said that the speech to inform is made up of a multitude of paragraphs devoted to different purposes. In some informative speeches, especially one on a technical or abstract subject, it is necessary to begin by defining ambiguous words, phrases, and expressions. In some informative speeches, it is necessary to describe; in others, it is necessary to analyze cause and explain process. Common sense and the nature of your subject should determine exactly what kinds of oral paragraphs you use. Here, for example, is an informative speech on botulism. Like all speeches to inform, this one is made up of a variety of different paragraphs, each devoted to a different purpose. We have labeled the paragraphs to indicate the approximate purpose they serve in the speech. Intended as a model of the typical speech to inform, this example illustrates how a speaker fashions oral paragraphs into a cohesive, informative speech.

BOTULISM—THE DEADLIEST POISON IN THE WORLD

Opening paragraph uses anecdotes to arouse interest.

Central idea of speech

1. The year is 1793; the place, Wildbad, Germany. Thirteen German peasants have just eaten a single sausage. Within hours, all are severely ill; within days, six are dead. The year is 1977; the place, Pontiac, Michigan. Diane Sprenger, a twenty-six-year-old nurse, has just eaten a mini-nacho—peppers and cheese on corn chips—at a Mexican restaurant. The next day, she is on a respirator, battling for her life. She is stricken with the same mysterious sickness that killed the six German peasants 184 years earlier. Its name is botulism, and it is the deadliest poison on earth.

Definition paragraph. Student uses etymological explanation to help define botulism.

2. What is botulism? Botulism is poisoning caused by the toxin of the bacteria *Clostridium botulinum*. *Clostridium* is Latin for "little spindle," which is what the bacterium looks like under a microscope; *botulinum* comes from *botulus*, the Latin word for "sausage," the food in which the poison first made its appearance. *Clostridium botulinum* is an ancient life form, billions of years old. It is an anaerobe, an organism that cannot survive in oxygen. The bacterium therefore lives deep in the soil, where air cannot penetrate. There, among the dark, airless, lightless dungeons of the soil, *Clostridium botulinum* ekes out a meager existence by breaking down chemicals from the soil for its food. In such a state, it is harmless to humans. We often breathe it into our lungs with dust; sometimes we swallow it with our food. But it does us no harm.

Paragraphs 3, 4, and 5 have as their prime purpose an explanation of the process of botulism contamination. Notice how the student illustrates this process by the use of a hypothetical example.

3. But during times of drought, when the soil dries up and blows as dust, *Clostridium botulinum* forms a shell around itself to shield it from the deadly effects of oxygen. This shell, called a pellicle, completely insulates the organism. Curled up inside its shell, in a state of microscopic hibernation, the bacterium is barely alive.

4. Then something happens. The bacterium, blown about with dust, lands on a green bean. The green bean is picked up by a housewife, who cans it. She boils the bean, and seals it in a jar. She thinks that by boiling, she has killed all the harmful bacteria. But she has not killed the *Clostridium* bacterium. Because of its shielding pellicle, *Clostridium* can withstand a half hour's boiling; it can survive freezing temperatures approaching absolute zero. The canned beans provide a perfect, oxygen-free environment for *Clostridium*. Mysteriously, the organism knows when it is safe to come out. Dissolving its pellicle, the bacterium awakens from its deathlike sleep.

5. Now it engages in a mysterious chemical process, something it doesn't do in the soil. It produces a toxin. The toxin is easily broken down by heat. Two minutes at 70°C destroys it. Even the actively living bacterium is now heat-sensitive. Two minutes over the stove kills it. But if the beans are eaten cold, and the toxin ingested, the results are often lethal.

Mixed paragraph. Primary aim is to describe the toxicity of the *botulinum* poison. However, student uses a contrast to achieve this description.

6. How toxic is the botulism toxin? Toxicologists base toxicity on six commonly used measures such as a taste, a mouthful, an ounce. A poison is rated as super-toxic if a taste, less than seven drops, or about 5 mg, can kill. Cyanide and strychnine are classified as super-toxic, since 5 mg of either is lethal. In contrast, 0.00015 mg of the botulism toxin is lethal. The botulism toxin, in other words, is 34,000 times more deadly than cyanide. Isaac Asimov, the well-known science writer, says that less than an ounce of *Clostridium botulinum*, properly distributed, could kill every man, woman, and child on the face of the earth.

Descriptive paragraph. Notice the dominant impression of botulism poisoning— "sudden, paralyzing, and difficult to diagnose." Details in the paragraph expand on this dominant impression.

7. The onset of botulism poisoning is sudden, paralyzing, and difficult to diagnose. Within six to ten hours after eating the beans, you have trouble focusing your eyes. The toxin has been absorbed into your bloodstream, where it is now attacking your nerve endings, blocking the transmission of impulses from the brain. You can't focus your eyes because your eye muscles are becoming paralyzed. Soon you can't swallow; you can't move your limbs. Then the respiratory muscles go. Conscious but paralyzed, you slowly suffocate to death. If botulism is diagnosed before paralysis sets in, you have a chance of being treated with antitoxins. But botulism is usually not diagnosed. The physician will probably think that you have polio, myasthenia gravis, or hysterical paralysis, all of which botulism poisoning resembles. Once paralysis has set in, forget about the doctor. Call a priest. Within a day or two, you'll be dead.

Conclusion. What can be done about it? Student ends speech by coming back to central idea—that botulism is the deadliest poison on earth.

8. How can botulism be avoided? The commonest source of botulism poisoning is home-canned food. Before you can any food, get a pamphlet on canning from the Government Printing Office and follow its instructions to the letter. Cook the food in a pressure cooker. Cook at 124°C (248°F) in moist heat. Never eat any home-canned or home-preserved food unless you're absolutely certain that the food was properly processed. Only by taking the strictest precautions with home-processed food can you escape falling victim to botulism—the deadliest poison in the world.

Review of applications

All speeches are made up of oral paragraphs. The informative speech usually consists of oral paragraphs that narrate, define, describe, divide and classify, compare and contrast, explain process, and analyze cause. Narrative paragraphs tell a story and are often used to make an issue appealing. Defining paragraphs specify the meanings of words and phrases. Descriptive paragraphs depict something through the use of a dominant impression and supporting details. Division and classification paragraphs break down a subject into its principal parts. Comparison/contrast paragraphs show how two items are alike or unalike. Process oral paragraphs give instructions or explain a sequence. And causal analysis paragraphs specify why something happened or analyze the effects of an event. Speakers also use paragraphs of mixed purpose that perform more than one of these functions. The point is not to imitate the paragraph structures of other speakers slavishly, but to use your own language to communicate as effectively as possible.

III. CAUTIONS

Not all oral paragraphs are equally easy to construct. It is generally harder to analyze cause than to define meaning, to compare and contrast than to explain process. Yet experience has shown that certain kinds of paragraphs are associated with certain common errors.

A frequent error that beginning speakers make with the defining paragraph is *overuse*. You should define only those words, phrases, or expressions whose meanings are ambiguous, controversial, technical, or abstract. For example, if you were giving an informative speech on how to ski, it would be unnecessary to define skiing. In the speech about botulism, the term is defined because most listeners would not be expected to know much, if anything, about the disease. In sum, you should define any difficult or unfamiliar word or term that is crucial to your topic, or any word or term used in a special sense—for example, Roger's use of the word *congruence* (page 180). But you should not define ordinary and unambiguous terms.

In constructing descriptive oral paragraphs, you should avoid using involved metaphors, complicated analogies, and exotic adjectives. Simple, easily understood metaphors can be used, along with short, easily grasped analogies. The vast army of insipid adjectives— *nice, cute, pretty, sweet, awful*—should be shunned. Each descriptive oral paragraph should be constructed around a single dominant impression, which supporting details in the paragraph should then develop.

The commonest errors in division and classification are based upon faulty thinking. The division is either not derived from a single principle or is incomplete. As an example of the first of these two errors—when the division is not based on a single principle—consider this proposed division of poetry:

Types of poetry:　　　　I. The epic
　　　　　　　　　　　II. The lyric
　　　　　　　　　　　III. The ballad
　　　　　　　　　　　IV. Eighteenth-century poetry
　　　　　　　　　　　V. The dramatic monologue

Eighteenth-century poetry—the fourth entry—does not belong in a division based on formal types of poetry. The category of eighteenth-century poetry would be appropriate—along with Renaissance and Victorian poetry—if the division had been based on chronological periods. As it stands, the division is based on two principles and is highly confusing.

A second common error is when the division is incomplete.

Classification of students:　I. Freshmen
　　　　　　　　　　　　　II. Sophomores
　　　　　　　　　　　　　III. Seniors
　　　　　　　　　　　　　IV. Graduates

Obviously, one important category is missing—juniors. The error is glaringly evident here; in more complicated divisions, it would not be as obvious. Consider, for instance, this division of Samuel Johnson's works:

Samuel Johnson's works:　I. Poetry
　　　　　　　　　　　　　II. Moral essays
　　　　　　　　　　　　　III. Literary criticism

Two important categories have been ommitted: Johnson's translations, for which he first became renowned, and his dictionary, for which he is perhaps best remembered. A general audience would perhaps not catch the omission, but any Johnson buff immediately would.

Finally, there is the venial error in division, when a speaker divides a subject into overlapping categories. Here is just such an error:

Kinds of love　　　　　I. Romantic love
　　　　　　　　　　　II. Conjugal love
　　　　　　　　　　　III. Parental love
　　　　　　　　　　　IV. Christian love
　　　　　　　　　　　V. Erotic love
　　　　　　　　　　　VI. Love in an open marriage

"Erotic love" can, perhaps, stand as a separate category, but "Love in an open marriage" cannot, since it is a variant of "Conjugal love." Overlapping categories do no serious harm to the intellectual integrity of a speech, but they make speeches longwinded and boring.

In giving a speech to inform, it is highly probable that you will have to devise oral paragraphs that divide and classify. Common sense dictates that you do the following in such paragraphs. First, devote a separate paragraph to each division. Notice, for instance, that the paragraphs on page 183 deal separately with divisions of venereal diseases, stages of syphilis, and stages of gonorrhea. Second, make the division according to a single principle. If the principle does not yield enough applicable categories, find another principle to base the division on. Third, make the categories mutually exclusive—that is, check all divisions to be sure that you're not repeating information in one category that is already covered in another. Finally, make the division complete. An incomplete division may bamboozle some members of the audience but not all. In any case, the speech containing an incomplete division will misinform rather than inform about a subject.

Possibly the most difficult of all paragraphs to construct are those that analyze cause and effect. The problem is that cause and effect are complex phenomena. Oral paragraphs analyzing cause must link a series of complicated propositions in a way that is immediately understandable to the audience. This is not at all easy to do and can result in a longwinded speech. Moreover, causal analysis—whether in an oral paragraph or in an entire speech—is always subject to logical breakdowns or to oversimplification.

When delivering oral paragraphs that explain cause, you can take the following precautions to avoid being illogical or being misunderstood. First, always use words and phrases that indicate clearly whether you are analyzing cause or deducing effect. If you are asserting that one thing is the cause of another, say so. Use expressions such as *because of, the reason for, the cause is,* which set up a causal connection. If you are deducing effect, you should likewise say so. Use expressions such as *the effect of this, in consequence of, as a result,* which plainly establish the relationship of effect you are asserting between two propositions.

Second, if the phenomenon has several causes, beware of discussing them within a single paragraph. Cause is a complex enough relationship to explain in a speech. If you cram the explanations of several causes into a single paragraph, your audience will surely be baffled. It is better to enumerate each cause separately and to amplify each within different paragraphs. For an example of this, turn to Chapter 9, pages 115–16, where the speaker enumerates in separate paragraphs the reasons for the increased incidence of venereal disease.

Third, avoid the use of circular or ideological reasoning in assigning cause. Circular reasoning occurs when a proposition intending to assert cause simply repeats itself. For instance, the statement "Smog is caused by air pollution" is circular, since it says, in effect, that air pollution causes air pollution. Ideological reasoning results when speakers possess special beliefs that they are eager to assign as primary causes. For instance, the speaker who asserts that "The high divorce rate in America is caused by the unwillingness of people to be 'born again' " is guilty of ideological reasoning. Causes, like facts, should be nonsectarian, nondenominational, and neutral; any cause that requires the acceptance of some special ideological belief is immediately suspect.

Finally, in analyzing cause, you should always turn your attention to the proximate, rather than to the remote, causes. Some mystics and philosophers have insisted that everything is the cause of everything else. Insurance investigators, taking the opposite tack, distinguish between proximate and remote cause. *Proximate cause* is the cause most immediate to the event; *remote cause* is the cause most distant from it. For instance, a stockbroker involved in a car accident may have been distracted by recent reversals in the stock market; but the actual cause of the accident may have been brake failure. Reversals in the stock market and their effect on the stockbroker would therefore be a remote cause of the accident; the proximate cause would be brake failure.

Review of cautions

Experience has shown that some common errors are associated with certain types of oral paragraphs. Beginning speakers tend to overuse defining paragraphs. In constructing descriptive paragraphs, they tend to use too many insipid adjectives. In dividing and classifying, they often do not base the division on a single principle; frequently they create incomplete divisions; occasionally, they divide a subject into overlapping categories. Causal analysis paragraphs are the hardest to construct because of the difficulty in analyzing cause. To analyze cause logically, a speaker must use words and phrases that clearly specify intent; must discuss different causes in separate paragraphs; must avoid ideology in assigning cause-and-effect relationships; and must concentrate on the proximate, not the remote, cause.

NOTES

[1] Carl Rogers, "What We Know About Psychotherapy—Objectively and Subjectively," California Institute of Technology, Spring 1960.

[2] Ralph Zimmerman, "Mingled Blood," Interstate Oratorical Contest, 1955.

[3] Mary Katherine Wayman, "The Unmentionable Diseases," Indiana University, Bloomington, Indiana, Summer 1967.

[4] Martin Luther King, Jr., "Love, Law, and Civil Disobedience." Fellowship of the Concerned, November 1961.

[5] Jenkins Lloyd Jones, "Who Is Tampering with the Soul of America?" Inland Daily Press Association, Chicago, Illinois, 16 October 1961.

[6] Charles Schalliol, "The Strangler," Interstate Oratorical Association contest, Bloomington, Indiana, 1967.

[7] Jones, "Who Is Tampering with the Soul of America?"

[8] Winston Churchill, "Civilization," address as Chancellor to the University of Bristol, England, 2 July 1938.

FOR FURTHER READING

Dillon, George L. *Constructing Texts.* Bloomington: Indiana University Press, 1981.

Gronbeck, Bruce E. *The Articulate Person: A Guide to Everyday Public Speaking.* Glenview, Ill.: Scott, Foresman, 1979.

Hirsch, E. D., Jr. *The Philosophy of Composition.* Chicago: University of Chicago Press, 1977.

Jones, Linda Kay. *Theme in Expository Discourse.* Lake Bluff, Ill.: Jupiter Press, 1977.

Kinneavey, James L. *A Theory of Discourse.* Englewood Cliffs, N.J.: Prentice-Hall, 1971.

Netter, Gwynn. *Explanations.* New York: McGraw-Hill, 1970.

Scholes, Robert, and Klaus, Carl. *Elements of Writing.* New York: Oxford University Press, 1972.

14

The speech to persuade

I. PRINCIPLES

A persuasive speech is a speech that tries to influence or change the beliefs of an audience. Generalizations about why such speeches are effective or ineffective are difficult to make. First, we do not completely understand how people think, and form beliefs and attitudes, and we do not understand why they change them. Much of what is known about attitude change is theoretical and murky and varies dramatically from one school of thought to another. Second, a great deal of information about the most effective tactics of persuasion is contradictory. We know for certain that some speakers are more persuasive than others. But we do not completely understand why, and we cannot yet give a foolproof prescription for persuasiveness. The variables are simply too many.

But, obviously, some speakers are more persuasive than others—an observation virtually no one would dispute. Speakers are said to be credible, charismatic, dynamic—epithets that denote the willingness of an audience to accept their word at face value. Other speakers are regarded in exactly the opposite way, not meriting belief, approval, or attention. Why? What makes one speaker believable and persuasive, and another dull and unconvincing?

Various answers have been suggested although none are definitive. Basically, however, an argument will persuade us for one of three reasons: (1) We are taken by the speaker's character; (2) we are impressed by the speaker's reasoning; (3) there is something in the argument for us.

The speaker's character

Consider, for instance, this situation. A single speech is tape-recorded and played back to three groups of students. One group is told that the speech is by the Surgeon General of the United States; the second group, that it is by the Secretary General of the Communist Party in America; the third group, that it is by a university sophomore. The same speech was then rated by all three groups of students. The group who thought that they had been listening to the Surgeon General rated the speaker significantly more competent than did the other two groups. Moreover, subsequent tests showed that the group most decidedly influenced by the speech was the group that thought it had heard the Surgeon General.[1]

Since all three groups had heard the same speech, it follows that some factor other than the wording or reasoning of the speech was responsible for its differing effect. This factor was labeled *ethos* by the ancient Greeks, their word for "character." *Ethos* refers to the perceived character of a speaker, and especially to its effect upon an audience. Aristotle (384–322, B.C.)—considered one of the greatest writers on rhetoric of all time—made the following observation of a speaker's character:

> The character of the speaker is a cause of persuasion when the speech is so uttered as to make him worthy of belief; for as a rule we trust men of probity more, and more quickly, about things in general, while on points outside the realm of exact knowledge, where opinion is divided, we trust them absolutely.[2]

Further, he added that the character of a speaker is "the most potent of all the means to persuasion."[3] To put it another way—all other things being equal, we believe the speaker whom we think credible. And where knowledge is inexact or controversial, we are especially inclined to follow the credible speaker.

Ethos, and its contribution to persuasion, has been much investigated, and Aristotle's speculations about its effects have been more or less confirmed. We are decidedly influenced by our impressions of a speaker's character. Studies have shown that children can be persuaded to eat foods they normally wouldn't eat if the food is endorsed by a fictional hero; that students can be persuaded to accept false descriptions of their personalities when told that the descriptions came from experts; that, in general, people have a tendency to shift their opinions to make them conform to views attributed to prestige sources.[4] If you have ever wondered about the rationale for having football players endorse car rental agencies, or movie stars rave about headache remedies, now you know.

The speaker's credibility　　What factors give a speaker *ethos,* make a speaker credible? Isolated in various studies, three components of ethos have been identified: competence, trustworthiness, and dynamism. Audiences rating speakers as credible often attribute these characteristics to them. Competent speakers are characterized by audiences as being "trained, experienced, qualified, skilled, informed, authoritative, able, and intelligent."[5] Speakers rated as incompetent are ascribed the opposites of these qualities. Trustworthy speakers are rated as kind, congenial, friendly, forgiving, hospitable, and so on; dynamic speakers are described as frank, emphatic, bold, forceful, energetic, and active.[6] Audiences attribute the opposite of these cataloged adjectives to those speakers variously described as untrustworthy or undynamic.[7]

Ethos, in sum, is the audience's judgment of a speaker's character and credibility. Moreover, as might be expected, such judgments tend to vary with the topic. A speaker judged as expert on one topic is not necessarily judged as expert on another.[8] A doctor, for instance, might be rated as expert on a medical topic but as unskilled on a topic of oceanography.

The speaker's values　　Apart from the *ethos* factor, we are also more likely to be persuaded by a speaker whom we take to be one of us. This peculiarity in audience reaction is known as the "assimilation/contrast effect." Basically, it says that audiences who perceive a speaker as possessing similar values to their own tend to exaggerate the similarity, while audiences who perceive a speaker as holding dissimilar values tend to exaggerate the disimilarity.[9] The exaggeration helps the speaker's case in the first instance, but hinders it in the second. Salespeople, for instance—whether peddling cars, houses, or books—often try to insinuate similarities between them and their clients to take advantage of this effect. Here is an oral paragraph in which a speaker stresses his similarity with an audience:

I must confess to a certain nostalgia on this great occasion. It was at this school over a generation ago that I had my first real contact with the world of ideas—with literature—with problem solving—with philosophic thought. It was here that I enjoyed close contact with a faculty which had some of the most competent, stimulating, and dedicated men it has ever been my privilege to know—men who have extended their own spiritual, intellectual, and moral heritage and influence far into posterity.[10]

The speaker's reasoning

We are also persuaded by the quality of a speaker's reasoning. Speakers who reason by documentation, support, and authority citation are more persuasive than speakers who merely generalize.[11] If you wish to persuade, you must therefore tell not just *what* you think but also *why* you think so, and what evidence exists that supports your thinking.

Reasoning is an attempt to give logical and accurate descriptions of the things, events, ideas, and experiences that make up reality. None of us can ever be sure that our version of reality is exactly shared by anyone else. In communication with another person, however, we do our utmost to explain what we perceive and why we perceive it. We swap ideas and notions; we make assertions about the relationships between things, ideas, experiences, and events. We classify assertions as true or untrue.

To simplify such exchanges, logic was invented. Basically, logic provides us with a neutral and unbiased language for describing reality. The language of logic contains built-in safeguards against exaggeration and deceit; it is universal and works for all known conditions. The opposite of logic is mysticism, magic, or some other psychic manifestation. But the flaw of such systems is that they rely exclusively on the individual's personal and unique powers. Logic does not. Logical discourse is the most democratic of all human transactions. Logic asks only three things of a reasoner: clarity, consistency, and proof. The requirement of clarity means that all assertions about reality must be stated with precision. Consistency requires that logical transactions be impartial and unswerving. Proof insists that logical assertions about ideas, events, experiences, or things must be supported by evidence.

Essentially, a logical description of reality is one that makes an accurate assertion either that a proposition is true or false, or that certain relationships exist between ideas, things, events, and experiences. Here, for instance, is an oral paragraph that first makes an assertion and then proves it:

> Public ignorance is especially troublesome. Everyone generally feels that students who say they will commit suicide never do. This simply isn't true. Dr. Edwin S. Sheidman and Dr. Norman L. Farberow of the Los Angeles Suicide Prevention Center made a study of suicide cases. They discovered that 75% of these people had given clear and certain indication of their intentions, either by word or deed, before they finally did end their lives. One Yale student talked of being "so very tired of life"—then shot himself to death. Students who make such remarks must be taken seriously.[12]

This oral paragraph satisfies our criteria for logic. Its assertions are clear and understandable. The student does not garble or misstate her assertion about students who threaten suicide. Having deduced that students who threaten suicide must be taken seriously, the speaker—to observe the requirement of consistency—must not argue or maintain the contrary anywhere else in the speech. For an assertion that is true in one part of a speech is also true in its other parts. Logical truth does not vary with the phase of the moon, the position of the planets, or the gravitational pull of the earth. Such circumstances may affect mystical truth, but their effect on logical truth is nonexistent.

Finally, the assertion about students who commit suicide is supported by proof. One may argue that the proof is insufficient, that the study was not thorough, that more investigation is needed before the truth of the assertion can be accepted. Logical propositions are not immune from different interpretations. But at least the process and the proof by which the speaker reached her conclusions are perfectly clear. Reasonable people now have something specific to argue reasonably about.

Appeals to self-interest

Unlike saints, most of us operate on the principle of self-interest. Arguments are especially appealing to us when they contain some proposals to our obvious benefit. The worker is rare, indeed, who could be persuaded to refuse a wage increase on the grounds that the refusal would help stem inflation. Most of us simply do not live on such a lofty, selfless plane.

What are the needs of audiences, and how do speakers appeal to them? Various attempts have been made to describe the needs of people. One such description, by the psychologist Abraham Maslow, classifies needs in a hierarchy:

1. *Physiological needs:* for the basics necessary to survive, such as food, drink, oxygen

2. *Safety needs:* for freedom from fear and harm, for security, protection, law, and structure

3. *Belongings and love needs:* for love and affection, for a feeling of membership in a group

4. *Esteem needs:* for self-esteem, recognition, status, prestige

5. *Self-actualization needs:* for being true to one's self; for becoming what one is potentially able to become

The theory is that each level of need has to be satisfied before the desires of the next level are felt. For instance, we obviously need food and air before we can begin to fret about safety; likewise, we must be safe and sheltered before we can worry about belonging.

If Maslow is right, then it follows that various need levels exist at which a speaker might aim the appeals of a speech. These need levels will vary with the audience. A well-fed, affluent audience is not likely to be moved by a speech appealing to the physiological needs of hunger. On the other hand, a hungry, poverty-stricken audience is likely to turn a deaf ear to a speech whose appeals are aimed at self-actualization needs. Much demagoguery—mindless, rabble-rousing appeals—has been directed at basic needs. Potential dictators and political firebrands are generally more successful in stirring up the mob when physiological or safety needs are threatened. People do not riot because they have been denied a chance at self-actualization; they riot because they are hungry, or because their safety is threatened. Appeals to the basic needs are extremely powerful.

The issues of argument

What is an *arguable* issue? Basically, it is an issue whose grounds for support exist outside the people arguing for or against it. This means that external evidence can be produced to support one side or the other. If the grounds of support are lodged entirely within the advocates themselves, the issue is circular and unresolvable. Let us say, for example, that you like American cars and your friend likes foreign cars. You may bicker about this difference, but you cannot prove that your *taste* is better than your friend's.

On the other hand, if you should contend that cars manufactured in America are safer than those made abroad, you have the basis of an arguable issue. Grounds of support for your contention can be found outside the realm of personal tastes. Various government agencies compile fatality statistics involving cars of different makes, and these statistics are available to the public.

Arguments, moreover, may involve one of three kinds of issues: propositions of fact, propositions of value, and propositions of policy. A *proposition of fact* primarily involves evidence and its interpretation. Generally, propositions of fact take the form of assertions that such-and-such is the case, or that such-and-such is not the case. For example, one of the recurring issues in the debate over capital punishment is a proposition of fact—whether or not capital punishment deters crime. Proponents of capital punishment say that it does deter crime; opponents say that it does not. Evidence exists on this point and arguments have raged over its interpretation.

A *proposition of value* involves a disputed value or goal. Suppose you contend that a certain Japanese car is better than a certain American car. The first question that must be answered is, What do you mean by "better"? To judge whether one thing is better than another, you must first decide on the criteria you will use in making the comparison. More profound issues may also be stated as propositions of value. For example, the argument over abortion is often phrased as a proposition of value: should the life of the fetus take precedence over the life of the mother?

Finally, there are *propositions of policy*. Policy is a way of dealing systematically and fairly with an issue. Propositions of policy are usually arguments about whether there ought to be a change in the way we deal with a problem or event. One argument raging in many states, for example, is whether existing laws against drunk driving are tough enough. Advocates of a change in policy must demonstrate that the present policy is harmful and that the change urged would be an improvement.

The beginning speaker may infer some useful lessons from this discussion. The first is that nearly all arguments are multifaceted. You could argue in favor of capital punishment as a proposition of fact—namely, that it is cheaper to execute incorrigible criminals than to maintain them in prison for life. This argument, though morally repugnant to some, has been advanced in some circles. On the other hand, you could argue against capital punishment as a proposition of value: some, for instance, have argued that capital punishment is morally wrong because it forces the state to commit the very crime it is supposed to deter. Implied in this line of reasoning is a proposition of value—that it is wrong for anyone, even the state, to take a human life.

The second lesson is that different kinds of propositions require different kinds of supporting details. Propositions of fact require the speaker to provide evidence and definition to back up the assertions being made. Propositions of value require a speaker to define and clarify the standards used in making a judgment. Propositions of policy require a speaker to show that the current policy is deficient or causes harm, and that a proposed change would be both practical and beneficial. In sum, the supporting detail for any argument must not only be specific and substantial; it must also be appropriate to the proposition being argued.

Review of principles

A persuasive speech tries to influence or change the beliefs of an audience. While it is difficult to say what makes one speech persuasive and another not, it is generally thought that audiences are persuaded by a speaker's character and reasoning, and by the appeals implicit in the speech. We are persuaded by a speaker we find believable or whose values coincide with our own; by the quality of the speaker's evidence; and by arguments appealing to our own self-interest. To be arguable, an issue must have grounds of support that exist outside the advocates themselves. Arguments generally involve three kinds of issues: propositions of fact, of value, and of policy. Propositions of fact are often assertions that revolve mainly around the interpretation of evidence. Propositions of value usually involve disputed goals. Propositions of policy urge changes in the way we systematically deal with a problem or an event. The difficult kinds of propositions often require different kinds of emphasis and supporting detail.

II. APPLICATIONS

The argumentative oral paragraph scarcely differs in structure from any other kind of oral paragraph. Basically, the speaker makes an assertion and then supports it with specific details. Here is an example:

> People can reduce and lose weight. Alfred Hitchcock went from 365 lbs. to a weight of 200 lbs. by eating only steak and cutting down on liquor; Jackie Gleason scaled down from 280 lbs. to 221 lbs. Maria Callas likewise went from a tumorous 215 lbs. to a trim 135 lbs. Even Lyndon Johnson, when he was vice president, lost 31 lbs. in less than 10 weeks after assuming the post in 1961.

In support of the assertion that weight loss is possible, the speaker cites the examples of four well-known people who have lost considerable weight.

All the advice and prescriptions we have given earlier about paragraph building apply as well to oral paragraphs intended principally to persuade. If you intend to say that one thing is the cause of another, do so with clear and conspicuous link words. Paragraphs that make fuzzy assertions simply do not convince. Nor, for that matter, do paragraphs that merely generalize. Persuasive arguments consist primarily of specific assertions documented with a wealth of convincing evidence. You must not only tell an audience *what* you wish them to believe; you must also tell them *why*.

There are other specific techniques that a speaker can use to make an argument more persuasive. Chief among them are the following.

Make your arguments logical

A logical argument asserts a true relationship between events, ideas, experiences, and things. Such relationships are typically of cause, consequence, category, alternative, or analogy. In a relationship of *cause,* a speaker simply proclaims one event as the cause of another:

> Air pollution is <u>caused</u> by dirty emissions from the ex hausts of automobile engines.

Assertions of *consequence* do just the opposite:

> Excessive spending by the federal government <u>results</u> in increased inflation.

Assertions of *category relationships* simply classify one item under the category of another:

> The dinosaur's high rate of metabolism and fast energy production <u>place</u> it not with the lizards but with the mammals and birds.

Therefore, all that is known about the category of mammals and birds applies as well to the dinosaur.

Assertions of *alternative* do not classify but relate ideas in an *either/or* formula:

> <u>Either</u> we stop polluting the atmosphere with freon <u>or</u> we face the prospect of increasing cases of skin cancer.

Assertions of *analogy* simply propose a likeness between two ideas, deducing from the outcome of the one, the outcome of the other:

> The kingdom of heaven is <u>like to</u> a grain of mustard seed, which a man took, and sowed in his field: Which indeed is the least of all seeds; but when it is grown, it is the greatest among herbs, and becometh a tree, so that the birds of the air come and lodge in the branches thereof.

In other words, as the mustard seed fares and spreads, so does the kingdom of heaven. Here is another, more scientific, argument by analogy:

> Generally, paleontologists have assumed that in the everyday details of life, dinosaurs were merely overgrown alligators or lizards. Crocodilians and lizards spend much of their time in inactivity, sunning themselves on a convenient rock or log, and, compared to modern mammals, most reptiles are slow and sluggish. Hence the usual reconstruction of a dinosaur such as *Brontosaurus* is as a mountain of scaly flesh which moved around only slowly and infrequently.

When attempts at logical argument fail, they generally do so for one of three reasons: They are unclear; they are inconsistent; they are unsupported. No effort will be made here to catalog every possible variation on these common errors. Unclear arguments, for instance, can be caused by any number of grammatical errors and oddities. Here is a proposition that is unclearly stated:

Poor: Studies show that the murder rates for police officers, guards, and private citizens are lower in states without the death penalty.

The implication of the assertion is that police officers, guards, and private citizens are doing the murdering.

Better: Studies show that the incidence of murder is lower in states without the death penalty.

Use accurate link words to express logical relationships

A chief cause of unclear assertions is the misuse of link words. Numerous words can be used to show the links between propositions, among them the following:

Link words that describe a relationship of cause

the cause of
because of
is caused by
is attributed to
is brought about by
is laid to

Link words that describe a relationship of consequence

in consequence of
therefore
thus
hence
the result of
is due to
since

Link words that describe a relationship of category

places it among
belongs to
can be classified under
is a member of
can be categorized with

Link words that describe a relationship of alternative

either . . . or
or

Link words that show a relationship of analogy

is like
can be compared to

> similarities exist between
> is analogous to

The list is by no means exhaustive, but these words are used most
often by writers and speakers to describe relationships between ideas,
events, experiences, and things. A common cause of muddled assertions is the misuse of link words. Here is an example:

> The theory of evolution is a complex idea wherein all liv-
> ing things are related to one another <u>since</u> they all come
> from the same common ancestor far back in geologic times.
> Through evolution, new species arise from preceding spe-
> cies of plants and animals that were simpler. This has been
> happening since plants and animals first existed on earth,
> and it is still going on. <u>Therefore,</u> all living things bear a
> relationship to one another and this is called the theory of
> evolution.

The link words are underlined. What muddles the assertion is the use
of two link words, when one would have been enough. Here is an
improvement on the assertion:

> The theory of evolution states that all living things are
> related through a common ancestor. New species of plants
> and animals are believed to have evolved from simpler
> species. Evolutionists contend that the process has always
> occurred and is still occurring, and that <u>consequently</u> all
> living things bear a relationship to each other.

It is now clear what two propositions are being described: the theory
of evolution and its consequences.

Make your arguments consistent

Inconsistency is another flaw of many arguments. A common
inconsistency occurs when a speaker asserts that one event is true in
one part of the speech and then assumes in another part that the
same event is false. A second, and more complicated, kind of inconsistency can exist between word and deed. Take the case of capital
punishment. A primary rationale for capital punishment is its supposed deterrence of crime. Potential criminals among us, frightened
by the gruesome fate of other criminals, are supposed to be deterred
from a life of crime. In the following passage, Albert Camus points

out the inconsistency between this belief and the actual practice of executions:

> To begin with, society does not believe what it says. If it really believed what it says, it would exhibit the heads [of guillotined criminals]. Society would give executions the benefit of the publicity it now generally uses for national bond issues or new brands of drinks. But we know that executions in our country, instead of taking place publicly, are now perpetrated in prison courtyards before a limited number of specialists.[13]

This kind of inconsistency is not technically a logical flaw, since nowhere among the canons of logic does it say that people must practice what they preach. Nevertheless, an inconsistency of this kind—between word and deed—can cast suspicion upon the strength and sincerity of an argument.

Establish your competence to speak on the subject

The status and prestige of a speaker cannot be altered for a speech, unless the speaker is willing to tell lies—which cannot be condoned. Yet the perceived competence of speakers also affects an audience's assessment of them, and it is possible for speakers to advertise their qualifications to an audience. Here is an oral paragraph in which a speaker tells an audience why he is qualified to talk about Malcolm X:

> I can remember a number of occasions when I talked to him, when I was with him, when I spoke on platforms with him; and so I am not indebted to printed material for my impressions of Malcolm X. I remember the last time he was in the city—not so much the speech, which was not one of his best by any means; it reflected, I think, much of the tension that he was under, much of the confusion, the constant living on the brink of violence. But I can remember him backstage, in the Gold Room I think they call it, of Ford Auditorium. Recently he had suffered smoke inhalation, the doctor had given him an injection, he was trying to sleep, he was irritable. But he was here because he had promised to be here, because he thought some people were concerned about what he had to say.[14]

Malcolm X had been dead for two years when this speech was given. In this paragraph, the speaker is obviously trying to establish his credibility by demonstrating, through detailed recollection, that he was personally acquainted with Malcolm X.

The point is that you will be more believable if the audience thinks you competent to give a speech on the subject. If you have a personal familiarity or experience with the subject, no harm can come of mentioning it. For example, if you are making a persuasive speech about the safety of hang-gliding and you have some personal experience with the sport, you should allude to it in your speech. Persuading your audience that you are something of an expert on the subject is bound to enhance your credibility in their eyes.

Appeal to the needs of your audience

In the persuasive speech, some oral paragraphs are constructed to appeal to the level of needs that are important to an audience. Such appeals are a legitimate part of persuasion and are often used by speakers. Here is one such oral paragraph, whose appeal is to the "security need":

> What we must not ignore is the desperate urgency of the need for undertaking a new approach to the problem of people-to-people communication. Not only in our Cold War struggle with communism, but also in our relations with such old and close friends as France and Canada, it is evident that the rhetoric of international communication has proved inadequate to the demands made upon it. No one, I think, will deny that the survival of our civilization, if not of the human race itself, may depend upon the speedy development of effective means of bridging culture gaps.[15]

Various other appeals are possible. For instance, if you were giving a speech urging that the school bookstore be taken over by the student union, you could appeal to students' needs to economize. Motivational appeals are most effective when they go right to the heart of an audience's primary need. Before drafting such oral paragraphs, you should analyze the needs of your audience and try to devise the kind of appeal that is most likely to have a strong effect.

Anticipate and answer opposing arguments

The ploy of anticipating objections to an idea and then answering them in a speech is routinely practiced by speakers. It is usually an effective tactic—especially if there are some commonly held and well-known arguments against a speaker's position. In the model speech at the end of this chapter, "Preventing Nuclear War," the speaker anticipates the "national security" argument usually raised against disarmament advocates and answers it:

> The need to re-examine assumptions about our foreign policy objective is also demonstrated by our self-centered definition of national security. Typically, political leaders and journalists alike suggest that the primary goal of foreign policy is national security, and only after that has been assured should we worry about our relations with the Soviet Union.
>
> Such thinking assumes that we can be secure while the Soviet Union is insecure—that somehow we can be safe while the Soviet Union faces a high risk of nuclear war. But in any nuclear war between the United States and the Soviet Union missiles will go both ways. There is no way we can make the world more dangerous for them without also making it more dangerous for ourselves. The less secure the Soviets feel, the more they will be doing about it, and the less secure we will become. Security is a joint problem.

Of course, a great deal of time cannot be spent on this sort of tactic or the speech will appear wholly negative. But if you can neatly sum up and effectively refute the main objections to your ideas, by all means do so.

Use emotional appeals

Appeals that play on hate, prejudice, or vengeance can never be condoned. Such appeals are the stock-in-trade of demagogues and rabble rousers. But emotional appeals that are directed at our better selves and that further an argument are legitimate. Here is an emotional appeal used by the philosopher Albert Camus in speaking against capital punishment:

Shortly before the war of 1914, an assassin whose crime was particularly repulsive (he had slaughtered a family of farmers, including the children) was condemned to death in Algiers. He was a farm worker who had killed in a sort of bloodthirsty frenzy but had aggravated his case by robbing his victims. The affair created a great stir. It was generally thought that decapitation was too mild a punishment for such a monster. This was the opinion, I have been told, of my father, who was especially aroused by the murder of the children. One of the few things I know about him, in any case, is that he wanted to witness the execution, for the first time in his life. He got up in the dark to go to the place of execution at the other end of town amid a great crowd of people. What he saw that morning he never told anyone. My mother relates merely that he came rushing home, his face distorted, refused to talk, lay down for a moment on the bed, and suddenly began to vomit. He had just discovered the reality under the noble phrases with which it was masked. Instead of thinking of the slaughtered children, he could think of nothing but that quivering body that had just been dropped onto a board to have its head cut off.

Presumably that ritual act is horrible indeed if it manages to overcome the indignation of a simple, straightforward man and if a punishment he considered richly deserved had no other effect than to nauseate him. When the extreme penalty simply causes vomiting on the part of the respectable citizen it is supposed to protect, how can anyone maintain that it is likely, as it ought to be, to bring more peace and order into the community? Rather, it is obviously no less repulsive than the crime, and this new murder, far from making amends for the harm done to the social body, adds a new blot to the first one.[16]

Camus' use of emotional appeal is temperate and an integral part of his argument—namely, that capital punishment is immoral. Moreover, the emotional appeal is not used in place of logic, but merely as a supplement to it. In his talk, he goes on to argue logically against the efficacy of capital punishment. The ethical use of emotional appeal depends on the speech and on the speech occasion. Universal rules are difficult to make, but it is surely not unreasonable to expect that speakers will use their emotional appeals temperately, and that they will use them, not in place of, but as a supplement to, logical arguments.

Review of applications

Although the argumentative oral paragraph is essentially the same in structure as the oral paragraph of any other kind of speech, speakers can and do use special techniques to persuade an audience. In making a persuasive speech, you should make your arguments logical; use accurate link words to express logical relationships; use consistent arguments; establish your competence to speak on the subject; appeal to the needs of your audience; anticipate and answer opposing arguments; and use emotional appeals ethically.

III. CAUTIONS

Our main caution is a warning to argue and persuade ethically. Ends do not justify means; you must play fair by sticking to the issues at hand and by dealing truthfully with evidence. Logicians have classified at length various kinds of unethical arguments that do not focus on arguable issues. Among these are the *ad hominem* argument—an attack against an opponent rather than an opponent's argument. Here is an example:

> My opponent, Mrs. Butler, favors the busing of children for the purposes of achieving racial integration. Naturally, she would take such a position. As everyone knows, she is a radical-liberal, and pinker than rare roast beef. Nothing would make her—or Moscow—happier than the destruction of our neighborhood schools.

Another illegitimate tactic of persuasion is the *red-herring* argument, which introduces a secondary, emotional issue that draws attention away from the real one. For instance, in an argument about whether schools should be allowed to lead children in group prayer, a speaker might say:

> The real question here is whether or not we intend to allow atheists to dictate school policy, whether or not we intend to allow atheists to run our children's lives.

That, of course, is not the question. Nor does it follow that an opponent of public school prayer is necessarily an atheist. But the assertion about atheists is so emotionally loaded that it is apt to distract from the real issue and put opponents of school prayer on the defensive. Ethical speakers do not stoop to such tactics.

Finally, there is the *ad populum* argument—an argument that appeals to passions and prejudices through the use of unflattering phrases to describe the position the speaker *opposes*. Conversely, the *favored* point of view is described in flattering terms and painted with patriotic colors. Here is an example:

> Many have spoken against the teaching of Darwinism and the theory of evolution in the schools, arguing that we must also teach so-called scientific creationism. But they fail to tell you the difference between the two. Darwinism and the theory of evolution is science; creationism is hocus-pocus. The theory of evolution was developed by a brilliant scientific mind and perfected through countless years of study. Creationism was dreamed up overnight in reactionary fervor. Those who stand for reason, truth, enlightenment, and progress stand behind the theory of evolution. Those who stand for creationism stand for the Dark Ages; the return of bell, book, and candle; the unreasoning groveling of the savage.

It is, of course, just as unethical to attack an issue in this way as it is to defame your opponent. To argue ethically, you must analyze the logic behind your opponent's views, point out inconsistencies, and explain evidence. It is unethical to attack your opponent personally, or to portray your opponent's position on an issue in purely derogatory terms.

Finally, you must never use evidence in an unethical way. Used ethically, evidence is not distorted, exaggerated, or misquoted. Speakers who are ethical will not use dated studies that have been replaced by later ones, will not misrepresent the credentials of an authority, and will not edit an opinion to make it appear more favorable to their views than it really is. No great moral or philosophical ambiguities are involved here. The point is merely to play fair with the audience, to share with them any conditions or stipulations that accompany the evidence you use.

Review of cautions

Our main caution is a warning to play fair with an audience. The ends of an argument do not justify the means. Ethical speakers do not use *ad hominem* arguments that direct an attack against a person rather than an issue; do not use *red herring* arguments that try to distract with a lurid and irrelevant issue; and do not use *ad populum* appeals to paint an opponent's position in unflattering terms. Nor do ethical speakers misrepresent the credentials of an authority, misquote an authority, or misuse evidence.

PREVENTING NUCLEAR WAR

Roger Fisher

Roger Fisher (1922–   ), professor of law at Harvard Law School, is the originator and executive editor of *The Advocates* (1969–1970) and *Arabs and Israelis* (1974–1975), two public-television series produced by WGBH in Boston. He is the author of several books, among them *International Conflict for Beginners* (1969) and *International Crises and the Role of Law: Points of Choice* (1978).

The following speech was delivered at a symposium organized by the Physicians for Social Responsibility on "The Medical Consequences of Nuclear Weapons and Nuclear War."

"Preventing Nuclear War"? "Boy, have *you* got a problem." That reaction a few minutes ago to the title of these remarks reminded me of an incident when during World War II, I was a B-17 weather reconnaissance officer. One fine day we were in Newfoundland test-flying a new engine that replaced one we had lost. Our pilot's rank was only that of flight officer because he had been court martialed so frequently for his wild activities; but he was highly skillful.

He took us up to about 14,000 feet and then, to give the new engine a rigorous test, he stopped the other three and feathered their propellers into the wind. It is rather impressive to see what a B-17 can do on one engine. But then, just for a lark, the pilot feathered the fourth propeller and turned off that fourth engine. With all four propellers stationary, we glided, somewhat like a stone, toward the rocks and forests of Newfoundland.

After a minute or so the pilot pushed the button to unfeather. Only then did he remember: In order to unfeather the propeller you had to have electric power, and in order to have electric power you had to have at least one engine going. As we were buckling on our parachutes, the co-pilot burst out laughing. Turning to the pilot he said, "Boy, have *you* got a problem!"

As with the crew of that B-17, we're all in this together. Professionals, whether lawyers like myself or doctors like you, tend to put the problem of preventing nuclear war on somebody else's agenda. But whoever is responsible for creating the danger, we're all on board one fragile spacecraft. The risk is high. What can we do to reduce it?

There are two kinds of reasons for the high risk: hardware reasons and people reasons. We—and the military—tend to focus on the hardware: nuclear explosives and the means for their delivery. We think about the terrible numbers of terrible weapons. We count them by the hundreds, by the thousands and by the tens of thousands. There are clearly too many. There are too many fingers on the trigger. There are too many hands through which weapons pass in Europe, in the United States and in the Soviet Union.

Yes, changes should be made in the hardware. I believe we should stop all nuclear weapons production; we should cut back on our stockpiles. But even if we should succeed in stopping production, and even if we should succeed in bringing about significant reductions, there will still be thousands of nuclear weapons. We keep our attention on the hardware. The military think it is the answer; we think it is the problem. In my judgment it is not the most serious problem.

The U.S. Air Force and the U.S. Navy both have enough weapons to blow each other up; and they have disagreements. There are serious disputes between the Air Force and the Navy: disputes that mean jobs, careers; disputes that are sometimes more serious in practical consequences than those between the United States and the Soviet Union. But the two services have learned to fight out their differences before the Senate Appropriations Committee, before the Secretary of Defense, in the White House and on the football field.

The case of the Navy and the Air Force demonstrates, in a crude way, that the problem is not just in the hardware; it is in our heads. It lies in the way we think about nuclear weapons. And if the problem lies in the way we think, then that's where the answer lies. In Pogo's immortal phrase, "We have met the enemy and they are us."

The danger of nuclear war is so great primarily because of the mental box we put ourselves in. We all have working assumptions that remain unexamined. It is these assumptions that make the world so dangerous. Let me suggest three sets of mistaken assumptions about: (1) our goals, that is, the ends we are trying to pursue; (2) the means for pursuing those ends; and (3) whose job it is to do what.

•First, what are our goals? Internationally, we think we want to "win." We go back to primitive notions of victory. We look at a situation and we ask, "Who's winning?" But that is an area in which we must change our thinking. Internationally and domestically, we do not really want a system in which any one side—even our own—wins all the time. Yet this concept of "winning"—that there is such a thing and that it is our dominant objective—is one of our fundamental beliefs.

In fact, like a poker player, we have three kinds of objectives. One is to win the hand. Whatever it is we think we want, we want it now. We want victory. The second is to be in a good position for future hands. We want a reputation and chips on the table so that we can influence future events. In other words, we want power. Our third objective is not to have the table kicked over, the house burned down, or our opponent pull a gun. We want peace.

We want victory; we want power; we want peace. Exploding nuclear weapons will not help us achieve any one of them. We have to re-examine rigorously our working assumption that in a future war we would want to "win." What do we mean by "win"? What would our purpose be?

Last spring I gave the officers at the NATO Defense College in Rome a hypothetical war in Europe, and asked them to work out NATO's war aims. The "war" was presumed to have grown out of a general strike in East Germany, with Soviet and West German tanks fighting on both sides of the border. Deterrence had failed. I told the officers: "You are in charge of the hotline message to Moscow. What is the purpose of this war? What are you trying to do?" At first they thought they knew—win! Very simple. But what did that mean? What was the purpose of the war? They began to realize that NATO did not plan to conquer the Soviet Union acre by acre as the Allies had conquered Germany in World War II. They did not plan physically to impose their will on the Soviet Union. They were seeking a Soviet decision. That was the only way they could have a successful outcome.

With further thought they reached a second conclusion; they were not going to ask for unconditional surrender. That gave them a specific task: Just define the Soviet decision that would constitute success for NATO and that NATO could reasonably expect the Soviet Union to make. The officers worked through the day considering how the Russians probably saw their choice, how we wanted them to see it, and what kind of "victory" for us we could realistically expect the Soviet Union to agree to.

It turned out that the only plausible objective was to stop the war. "Winning" meant ending the war on acceptable terms. The goal was some kind of cease-fire, the sooner the better. It was with difficulty and even pain that some officers discovered that winning meant stopping, even if some Soviet troops remained in West Germany; even with only a promise to restore the *status quo ante*.

They found it hard to draft a fair cease-fire that didn't sound like a unilateral Western ultimatum. It might say, "Stop firing at 0100 hours tomorrow, promise to withdraw, promise to restore the status quo within 48 hours, and we will meet in Vienna to talk about serious problems as soon as the status quo is 'more or less' restored." But the NATO draftsmen did not know whether the Soviets would prefer Geneva to Vienna or whether they wanted 0200 hours instead of 0100 hours, etc.

Someone creatively suggested, "Wouldn't it be a good idea if right now we worked out with the Russians some standby cease-fire terms? Then in a crisis we wouldn't have to be demanding that they accept our terms or they demanding that we accept theirs. Let's produce some cease-fire drafts that we can both accept." One of the other officers was incredulous: "What did you say? You are going to negotiate the armistice before the war begins? In that case, why have the war?"

The need to re-examine assumptions about our foreign policy objectives is also demonstrated by our self-centered definition of national security. Typically, political leaders and journalists alike suggest that the primary goal of foreign policy is national security, and only after that has been assured should we worry about our relations with the Soviet Union.

Such thinking assumes that we can be secure while the Soviet Union is insecure—that somehow we can be safe while the Soviet Union faces a high risk of nuclear war. But in any nuclear war between the United States and the Soviet Union, missiles will go both ways. There is no way we can make the world more dangerous for them without also making it more dangerous for ourselves. The less secure the Soviets feel, the more they will be doing about it, and the less secure we will become. Security is a joint problem.

We must make the Soviet Union share responsibility for our security problem. We should say, "Look, you Russians have to understand why we build these missiles and how it looks to us when you behave as you do. You must take some responsibility for helping us deal with our security problem." Similarly, we must take on responsibility for dealing with their security problem. We cannot make our end of the boat safer by making the Soviet end more likely to capsize. We cannot improve our security by making nuclear war more likely for them. We can't "win" security from nuclear war unless they win it too. Any contrary assumption is dangerous.

Here I may point out that we in the peace movement do not always practice what we preach. I am always ready to tell friends at the Pentagon that it does no good to call Soviet officials idiots, but am likely to add, "Don't you see that, you idiot?" We who are concerned with reducing the risks of war often think that our job is to "win" the war against hawks. In advancing our interests we assume that our adversaries have none worth considering. But our task is not to win a battle. Instead, we have to find out what the other side's legitimate concerns are, and we have to help solve their legitimate problems in order to solve our own. At every level, domestically and internationally, we need to re-examine our working assumptions. We are not seeking to win a war, but to gain a peace.

•A second set of dangerous assumptions are those we make about how to pursue our objectives. The basic mistaken assumption is that for every problem there is a military solution. We will first try diplomacy. We will talk about it; we will negotiate. But if that doesn't solve the problem we assume that we can always resort to force. We tend to assume that if we have the will and the courage, and are prepared to pay the price, then we can always solve the problem by military means. Wrong. For the world's big problems there is no military solution. Nuclear war is not a solution. It is worse than any problem it might "solve."

We have mislearned from the past. During World War II the Allies could physically impose a result on Hitler and his country. Acre by acre it was done. But the world has changed. We can no longer impose such a result on any nuclear power. We cannot physically make things happen. The only means we have available is to try to change someone's mind.

There is no way in which nuclear hardware can bring about a physical solution to any problem we face except the population problem. Just as you cannot make a marriage work by dynamite or make a town work by blowing it up, there is no way we can make the world work by using nuclear bombs. When people hear that they say, "Yes, that's true." Yet they go right ahead, operating on the assumption that there are military solutions.

Like Linus in the Charlie Brown comic strip, we cling to our security blanket, military hardware. Both U.S. and Soviet officials clutch their plutonium security blankets as though somehow they offer real security. Somehow, we think, this bomb, this hardware, will give us strength, will protect us. We will be able to avoid the necessity of dealing with the real world. Our assumption is that the problem is simple—it's us against them. We want to believe in a quick fix. It is like cowboys and Indians. Whatever the problem, John Wayne will arrive with his six-guns blazing, and the problem will be solved.

Those are our common assumptions about how to deal with international problems. We operate on them although most of us know they are not true. The fact that conventional weapons remain useful and that conventional wars, such as that between Iraq and Iran, continue, reinforces our mistaken assumptions about the use of nuclear weapons.

We have far better ways to deal with international problems. Break up big problems into manageable pieces. Look at each item on its merits. Sit down side-by-side and discuss it. Don't concentrate on what our adversaries say their positions are, but try to understand and deal with their interests. Communicate and listen. What's in their minds? What's bothering them? How would we feel?

If you were sitting in Moscow and looking off to the left saw Japan thinking of rearming; if you saw your long-time strongest ally, China, with a 2,000-mile common frontier, now your worst enemy; if you saw Pakistan apparently getting a nuclear bomb; if you heard Western voices saying, "We must help the rebels in Afghanistan"; if you saw American military equipment now in the Gulf, in Saudi Arabia, in Egypt and in Israel; if you saw Greece rejoining NATO and Turkey in the hands of a military government; and if cruise missiles were about to be located in West Germany—how must that all look from Moscow? We should put ourselves in their shoes and understand their problems. The only way we can succeed is to affect their future thinking. The starting point is to understand their present thinking.

Second, we have to invent wise solutions. We have to figure out not just good arguments, but good ways to reconcile our differing interests. And they must participate in that process. There is no way, in any conflict, in which one side can produce the right answer. The understanding that comes from both sides working on a problem, and the acceptability that comes from joint participation in a solution, make any good answer better. We need to engage in joint problem-solving.

That same process of working together is equally applicable to our domestic differences. The peace movement is not the only source of wisdom; we are part of the conflict. There are a lot of people in this country who have legitimate concerns about the Soviet Union. We must try to understand these concerns and meet them, not carry on a war. We need to put ourselves in their shoes—in Pentagon shoes. We have to listen as well as talk. With their participation, we will invent better solutions.

By this process we will promote joint learning, not just at the intellectual level but at the level of feeling, of emotion, of caring, the level of concern. International conflict is too often dealt with cerebrally, too often dealt with as a hypothetical problem out there. We need not only to apply what we know, but to keep on learning about human behavior, how to affect our own behavior and that of others, not just manipulate it.

The danger of nuclear war lies largely within us. It lies in how we think about winning, in how we define success, and in our illusions of being able to impose results.

•The danger also comes from my third set of assumptions—about whose job it is to reduce the risk of war. If there were a military solution, there would be a case for leaving it to the military—to policy-science experts, and to professional strategists. Physicians, for example, have said: "We are just concerned with the medical aspects of nuclear war and will limit ourselves to that area. We will tell you how bad a nuclear war would be. It is somebody else's job to prevent it."

Such statements rest on the assumption that the solution is in the hardware department. But we are not facing a technical military problem "out there." The solution lies right here: in changing our own assumptions and those of other people; in growing up; in abandoning our plutonium security blanket.

The Soviet Union and the United States cling to nuclear weapons as symbols of security; other national leaders want them. If someone is clinging to a plutonium blanket which is bad for his health, you do not call in an engineer and say, "Design a better plutonium blanket." The problem is in the heads of those who are clinging to it.

There is no one I know who has a professional license in the skills of reducing the risk of nuclear war. Fortunately, however, no professional license is required. But who are those with skills in dealing with psychological problems like denial, like distancing, like turning flesh and blood issues into abstract problems through the use of jargon? Who is likely to notice that people are denying responsibility because a problem seems too overwhelming? Nuclear engineers? I think not.

A few minutes ago I left you in a B-17 over the hills of Newfoundland. The co-pilot was saying to the pilot: "Boy, do *you* have a problem." Well, we didn't crash; we weren't all killed. On that plane we had a buck sergeant who remembered that back behind the bomb bay we had a putt-putt generator for use in case we had to land at some emergency air field that did not have any electric power to start the engines. The sergeant found it. He fiddled with the carburetor; wrapped a rope around the flywheel a few times; pulled it and pulled it; got the generator going and before we were down to 3,000 feet we had electricity. The pilot restarted the engines, and we were all safe. Now saving that plane was not the sergeant's job in the sense that he created the risk. The danger we were in was not his fault or his responsibility. But it was his job in the sense that he had an opportunity to do something about it.

We professionals tend to define our roles narrowly. I sometimes ask my law students: "What would have been the responsibility of a professional musician judging Nero's performance on the fiddle while Rome burned? Should he limit himself to discussing the music?" A member of the lay public would probably get a bucket and put out the fire. By becoming professionals do we become less responsible? Can we say, "No, I'm a professional. I'm not a firefighter. That's someone else's job"?

Such special knowledge and training as we have may not make

it obligatory for us to try to prevent nuclear war. Rather, it gives us an opportunity. My notion of whose job something is is best defined by who has an opportunity. We have an opportunity. I encourage you, as I encourage myself, to use it. The world is at risk. The very danger of nuclear war means that there is more opportunity to make a difference than ever before.

If everyone with any significant power made the right decision every time, that's as near utopia as we can get. There are only three reasons they don't. One is that they are poor decision-makers. Our job is to change them; that is what politics is about. Second, they are operating on bad assumptions, thinking poorly. Our job is to correct their assumptions. And the third possibility is that they are subject to harmful constraints. Our job is to free them from those constraints.

In a simple chart I have put all problems on the left-hand side, divided into those three parts. Across the top are the activities in which we can engage: research on facts and theory; communication

Chart of useful activities

Avoiding nuclear war will require wise decision-makers, who make wise assumptions on ends and means, and who are free from harmful constraints. Which part of that problem do you want to work on? Which activity will best harness your interests and abilities? To get wise results someone must devote attention to each box in the matrix. To get a wise decision answers are needed in every box.

PROBLEMS	ACTIVITIES					
	Research: facts, theory	Commu- nicate: learn, teach	Devise things to do	Build an agenda	Advocate	Do it yourself
Poor deciders						
Poor thinking on ends on means						
Harmful constraints						

in terms of learning ourselves and teaching others; devising things to do (that is, turning a problem into a possible answer, inventing possible proposals or action ideas); getting a proposal onto somebody's agenda; advocating ideas; or doing something ourselves.

To get a wise decision we need good answers *in every box*. No amount of useful research will overcome poor deciders; no number of good deciders will overcome bad assumptions or harmful constraints. Somebody has to invent what's to be done. Somebody has to put it on the agenda. Somebody has to persuade others that it is a good idea and somebody has to do it. All those activities are needed for each category of problem. There is enough to keep all of us busy.

All of us can do any of those things. No single activity will be sufficient. We need theory on how to reduce instability. We need to develop knowledge about nuclear war, about the consequences and about ways to reduce the risks. We need to communicate that knowledge both to the public, who constrain our decision-makers, and to the people who are making the decisions. We need to communicate both the bad news and the opportunities for reducing it.

If all we do is deliver bad news and say that there's nothing we can do about it, the bad news does not become operational. We have to turn that news into something we can do.

My favorite activity is inventing. An early arms control proposal dealt with the problem of distancing that the President would have in the circumstances of facing a decision about nuclear war. There is a young man, probably a Navy officer, who accompanies the President. This young man has a black attaché case which contains the codes that are needed to fire nuclear weapons. I could see the President at a staff meeting considering nuclear war as an abstract question. He might conclude: "On SIOP Plan One, the decision is affirmative. Communicate the Alpha line XYZ." Such jargon holds what is involved at a distance.

My suggestion was quite simple: Put that needed code number in a little capsule, and then implant that capsule right next to the heart of a volunteer. The volunteer would carry with him a big, heavy butcher knife as he accompanied the President. If ever the President wanted to fire nuclear weapons, the only way he could do so would be for him first, with his own hands, to kill one human being. The President says, "George, I'm sorry but tens of millions must die." He has to look at someone and realize what death is—what an innocent death is. Blood on the White House carpet. It's reality brought home.

When I suggested this to friends in the Pentagon they said, "My God, that's terrible. Having to kill someone would distort the President's judgment. He might never push the button."

Whether or not that particular idea has any merit, there is lots to do. Action is required to convince the public that it is in our interest to have the Soviets feel secure rather than insecure. Much of the press apparently thinks that the more terrified the Soviets are the more we benefit. The Committee on the Present Danger (perhaps better called the Committee on Increasing the Present Danger) ignores the fact that if we raise the risk of nuclear war for the Soviet Union we also raise it for ourselves.

If you don't know what to do, that's great. That gives you something to do right there. Get some friends together on Saturday morning and generate some ideas. Separate this inventing process from the later process of deciding among them. Identify three or four other people who might make a decision of some significance. What can you do to increase the chance they'll make some desired decision next week? Whoever it is—journalists, congressmen, governors, legislators, newspaper editors, businessmen, a civic organization, a medical association, a friend of President Reagan's, a school teacher, a publisher—what are some things they might do that would illuminate our faulty working assumptions to help establish better ones? Figuring out what to do is itself an excellent activity. In intellectual efforts, as in gunnery, aiming is crucial.

Don't wait to be instructed. Take charge. This is not an organized campaign that someone else is going to run. If you share these concerns, get involved. There is a lot to do to reduce the risk of nuclear war. Reading, writing, talking, perhaps a radio program, or perhaps a letter-writing campaign to your congressman. Tell him, "Grow up. Give up your plutonium security blanket."

But perhaps you are still holding on to your own security blanket, that neat definition of your job. The security blanket most of us cling to is, "Don't blame me. It's not my job to plan nuclear strategy. I'm not responsible for the risk of nuclear war." You can give up that security blanket any time.

The way to enlist support is not to burden others with guilt but to provide them with an opportunity to volunteer. I find it an exciting venture. It is a glorious world outside. There are people to be loved and pleasures to share. We should not let details of past wars and the threat of the future take away the fun and the joy we can have working together on a challenging task. I see no reason to be gloomy about trying to save the world. There is more exhilaration, more challenge, most zest in tilting at windmills than in any routine job. Be involved, not just intellectually but emotionally. Here is a chance to work together with affection, with caring, with feeling. Feel some of your emotions. Don't be uptight. You don't have to be simply a doctor, a lawyer, or a merchant. We are human beings. Be human.

People have struggled all of their lives to clear ten acres of ground or simply to maintain themselves and their family. Look at the opportunity we have. Few people in history have been given such a chance—a chance to apply our convictions, our values, our highest moral goals with such competence as our professional skills may give us. A chance to work with others—to have the satisfaction that comes from playing a role, however small, in a constructive enterprise. It's not compulsory. So much the better. But what challenge could be greater? We have an opportunity to improve the chance of human survival.

In medicine there is a traditional call that strikes a nice balance between duty and opportunity, that invites us to lend a hand with all the skill and compassion we can muster: "Is there a doctor in the house?"

NOTES

[1] Kenneth Andersen and Theodore Clevenger, Jr., "A Summary of Experimental Research in Ethos," *Speech Monographs* 30 (June 1963): 62–63.

[2] *The Rhetoric of Aristotle,* trans. Lane Cooper (Englewood Cliffs, N.J.: Prentice-Hall, 1960), p. 8.

[3] *The Rhetoric of Aristotle,* p. 9.

[4] Andersen and Clevenger, p. 77.

[5] Erwin P. Bettinghaus, *Persuasive Communication* (New York: Holt, Rinehart & Winston, 1968), p. 106.

[6] Bettinghaus, *Persuasive Communication,* p. 106.

[7] Bettinghaus, *Persuasive Communication,* pp. 106–107.

[8] Bettinghaus, *Persuasive Communication,* p. 108.

[9] Donovan J. Ochs and Ronald J. Burritt, "Perceptual Theory: Narrative Suasion of Lysias" in *Explorations in Rhetorical Criticism,* ed. G. P. Mohrmann, Charles J. Stewart, and Donovan J. Ochs (University Park, Pa.: The Pennsylvania State University Press, 1973), p. 62.

[10] Gerald J. Lynch, "The Pursuit of Security," University of Dayton, Dayton, Ohio, December 1963.

[11] Andersen and Clevenger, "A Summary of Experimental Research," p. 71.

[12] Patricia Ann Hayes, "Madame Butterfly and the Collegian," Indiana Oratorical Association contest, Bloomington, Indiana, 1967.

[13] Albert Camus, "Reflections on the Guillotine," from a symposium with Arthur Koestler, Paris, France, 1957.

[14] Albert Cleage, "Myths About Malcolm X," speech given in Detroit, Michigan, 24 February 1967.

[15] Robert T. Oliver, "Culture and Communication," University of Denver, Denver, Colorado, 1963.

[16] Albert Camus, "Reflections on the Guillotine."

FOR FURTHER READING

Brockriede, Wayne, and Ehninger, Douglas. *Decision by Debate.* New York: Dodd, Mead, 1963.

———. "Toulmin on Argument: An Interpretation and Application." *Quarterly Journal of Speech* 46 (February 1960):44–53.

Cederblom, Jerry, and Paulsen, David. *Critical Reasoning.* Belmont, Calif.: Wadsworth, 1982.

Cronkhite, Gary. "The Locus of Presumption." *Central States Speech Journal* 17 (November 1966):270–276.

Ehninger, Douglas. "Argument as Method: Its Nature, Its Limitation, and Its Uses." *Speech Monographs* 37 (June 1970):101–110.

Fahnestock, Jeanne, and Secor, Marie. *A Rhetoric of Argument.* New York: Random House, 1982.

McKerrow, Ray E. "Rhetorical Validity: An Analysis of Three Perspectives on the Justification of Rhetorical Argument." *Journal of the American Forensic Association* 13 (Winter 1977):133–141.

Nosich, Gerald M. *Reasons and Arguments.* Belmont, Calif.: Wadsworth, 1982.

Toulmin, Stephen. *The Uses of Argument.* London: Cambridge University Press, 1958.

Weddle, Perry. *Argument: A Guide to Critical Thinking.* New York: McGraw-Hill, 1978.

Ziegelmueller, George W., and Dause, George. *Argumentation: Inquiry and Advocacy.* Englewood Cliffs, N.J.: Prentice-Hall, 1975.

Index